The (Almost) Christmas Baby

Perry Coleman Dupuis

THE (ALMOST) CHRISTMAS BABY

This book is written from my recollections of true events and I have tried to recreate details, locations and conversations from my memories of them. Some names and identifying details have been changed to protect the privacy of individuals.

Formatting by Rik: Wild Seas Formatting

Cover - copyright LP Designs & Art

ISBN: eBook - 978-1-7775636-0-8

ISBN: print - 978-1-7775636-1-5

CONTENTS

ACKNOWLEDGEMENTS

Sincere thanks to my dear friend Gill Douglas-Mann for first encouraging me to write this book. She is a pit-bull when it comes to the English language, and what better person to read and edit the first rough draft. Without her positive feedback I would never have put this story down on paper.

After it was drafted, the manuscript sat for ten years until I was ready to think about publishing. I had reconnected with an old friend, Barbara Neill - herself a published author - and she agreed to read and edit the manuscript for me. She encouraged me to self-publish and made me realize that the time was finally right.

My thanks to Rik Hall for formatting the manuscript and answering my newbie author questions.

Thanks also to Liz Ponting of LP Designs & Art for her expertise with the cover design.

I am extremely grateful to Sue Davies at Making Connections, who buoyed me up during some low times and arranged for a short piece to be published about my search in their magazine. She made me see it was important to write the story in its entirety.

My dear mum Iris has since passed away, but she was right there with me as I was writing this book. Without her openness, love and approval this would never have been written. And without her and my wonderful dad Fred, my life would have been very different.

I would like to thank Ellwood Hodgson for putting up with all the long evenings I spent on the computer and for generally holding me together during some of the rougher days.

And lastly to my daughters, this story is your story too. It's not all pretty but you deserve to know it, so thank you for allowing me to tell it.

EPIGRAPH

"The openness of our hearts and minds can be measured by how wide we draw the circle of what we call family."

- *Mother Teresa*

INTRODUCTION

Imagine this: it's a few days before Christmas and there's a newborn baby in your house. She's not your baby, but circumstances have put her there, swaddled in a blanket, in the wooden drawer sitting on your living room floor. You don't have much. You don't have a crib; you don't have anything for her. She's been left with you by her mother, who had to go back to her old life. She's just a few days old, tiny and helpless. What do you do? Call social services? What might happen to her if you do that? It's almost Christmas and you remember the story of Jesus being born in a stable. That's what Christmas is really about, isn't it? And here's a baby that needs help, right here in your home. It's suddenly obvious what you need to do. This baby needs a place to stay and people to love her. You will take her in, and you will keep her for as long as it takes. You will make sure she is safe. Then, when she is ready to leave, you will send her off with love to start the journey of her life. This is where the story of The (Almost) Christmas Baby begins.

Many adopted people struggle with rejection. I did, and I still do to some extent, but I believe that being loved from the very beginning of my life allowed me to grow up without that feeling of abandonment that so many adult adoptees struggle with. I've not done so well with some significant relationships but that may have been more because I made some poor choices early on, which led me into less-than-ideal situations. That's for another book. But the fact remains that attachment disorders are a very real thing for adopted people, and they suffer because bonding with another human being on an intimate level just isn't possible. I've discovered that I was unusually blessed because, although I wasn't with my birth mother, I was loved from the very beginning of my life. Firstly by the family that took me in, and then by one of the nannies at the children's home where I was eventually placed, who took a special interest in me. I was therefore able to grow into adulthood with less bonding issues than many other adoptees and I find that very profound. Love is a powerful thing. Interestingly, it doesn't seem to matter who does the loving, or even if the person loving the child changes; it is the continuous genuine nurturing love that's important, not who gives it.

Before I embarked on my search journey, amongst other things I wanted to understand the circumstances that led to me being given up. I also had a feeling of not quite belonging where I found myself and I felt I was quite different from my adoptive family. Not only physically, but I had very different personality traits, mannerisms and behaviours. I think these are common feelings that adopted people have. By researching, I did find some answers to these questions and gained an understanding of the disturbing societal pressures of the day, back in the 1950's, which wreaked emotional havoc upon unmarried mothers. I feel that thankfully we have moved on a good deal in our attitudes since those days, and women are no longer counselled by social workers to walk away from their children and forget they even existed, and to do all that with no ongoing counselling or support. That is not to say that sometimes family pressure still exists in some cases to do just that, so it does still happen.

After finding my biological families, my feeling of not quite belonging where I found myself was somewhat resolved, but I also saw first-hand that my life would have been very different had I not been given up, and that my birth mother had made the right choice, even if she didn't know it. I don't know how much she knew of my biological father's family situation; probably not much, but certainly the nurture component of making me who I am as an adult would have been very different. As for the nature component, the physical likeness and even mannerisms and traits inherited from my birth family, particularly on my father's side, are very compelling.

I wanted to write this book firstly so that my children would have a record of the story - notice I don't call it "my story" because it very much belongs to everyone I found along the way, too - as it is their heritage as well as mine. Later, I realized that my somewhat convoluted journey might help and encourage other people who have been adopted or fostered to find their way, either by tracing their roots or re-establishing contact with their biological families. It's not all about meeting biological parents; there are siblings, grandparents, aunts and uncles, and all manner of other people who may be wanting to know more about you or have questions themselves that need to be answered. You may be able to do that for them. Mine wasn't a pretty journey but it helped me to understand that there is always a bigger picture and that we are not alone in needing healing and reconciliation.

Times have already changed since I started my search journey more than ten years ago. There has been a surge of interest in ancestry, family history, and finding long lost relatives. It seems to have captured the collective imagination of society. Television shows like Long Lost Family and Who Do You Think You Are? have brought family reconciliations into the living rooms of the nations. Of course, it's not always the perfect ending, as one of my biological aunts wisely told me, "They're not all good endings, sometimes they're just endings," and there is some wisdom in that. Perhaps you are just looking for closure, and not an ongoing family relationship. If you want to start a search, genealogy websites like Ancestry, FamilySearch and Findmypast abound online. There are endless databases that can be searched, family trees that can be accessed or created, and even at-home DNA tests that can be submitted, matching you up with distant and not-so-distant relatives. You can even hire a professional researcher to do the work for you. It's really never been easier to track people down, so if the desire is there it can probably be done a lot quicker and easier than it could even just a few years ago. I know it's not for everybody, and I know sometimes it feels overwhelming, but I wrote this book because even though it's not always a happy ending, there are good things that come out of bad circumstances.

So if you're sitting on the fence, think about stepping off. I have no regrets and I hope you won't, either.

Perry Coleman Dupuis
January 2021

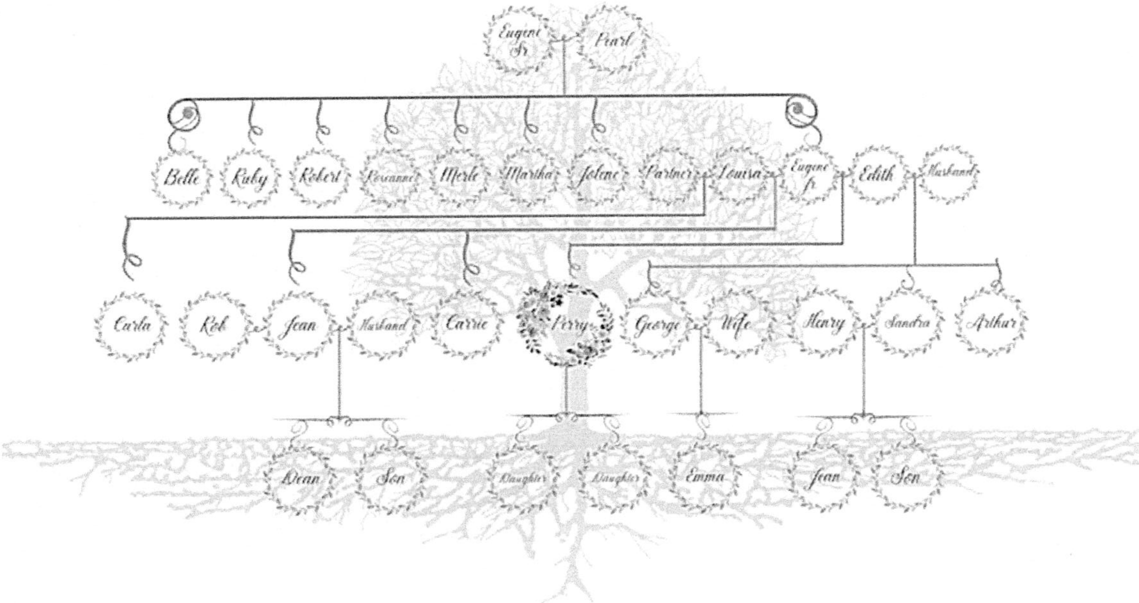
Eugene Sr
Pearl
Belle
Ruby
Robert
Roseanne
Merle
Martha
Jolene
Partner
Louisa
Eugene Jr
Edith
Husband
Carla
Rob
Jean
Husband
Carrie
Perry
George
Wife
Henry
Sandra
Arthur
Dean
Son
Daughter
Daughter
Emma
Jean
Son

1

The Early Days

This is what I knew. I was born in Norfolk, England in December 1958. I was an (almost) Christmas baby. I was named Perry Christina Keyes and I had been given up for adoption. I had spent some time at a children's home before I was adopted by Fred and Iris Coleman, a couple from London who could not have children of their own. They became my mum and dad.

Iris and Fred were good, traditional, upstanding people. They did their best for me and my younger adopted sister, who had landed in the family when I was about three years old. Fred, my dad, was a sales representative who had worked for the same company for almost all his working life, and Iris, my mum, stayed at home to look after us when we were young. They held very strongly to their solid family values.

It's hard to imagine now, but adoption was a very secret affair back in the 1950's, when it was seen as something less than savoury. It wasn't talked about and it was thought to only happen to the unfortunate children of prostitutes and Heaven forbid, unmarried mothers. The truth is that unwanted children came from all walks of life and all social classes, but nonetheless it was considered a shameful thing to be born out of wedlock, and an even more shameful thing to be the mother of one of those 'bastard children', as we were called. Thank God times have changed, but in those unenlightened times we were best hidden away and most definitely not talked about. For the lucky ones like me, who found a family, our shameful roots were expunged with the bang of the Judge's gavel, the paperwork signed, stamped and filed away and in those days, never intended to see the light of day again.

Mum and Dad believed that my adopted sister and I should both grow up knowing the truth; that we were not their natural children, but instead we had been gifted to them because our natural mothers were unable to keep us. For me, this was never an issue. I never felt any different from my friends, and I think as children things seem a lot less complicated. I just accepted what they told me. It was not quite the same for my sister, who I believe was profoundly affected by being given up for adoption. She felt somehow rejected and never wanted to hear anything about it.

Now I understand that this honesty was a brave step for Mum and Dad to take, and not just with us. Very often adoptive parents went to great lengths to conceal the fact that their children were not their natural offspring, and sometimes for good reason as it was often frowned upon even within their own families. Adoption agencies tried to match up physical characteristics of the children to those of prospective parents, hair and eye colour for example, so that it wouldn't be obvious that the child wasn't their own.

Many years later, I found out that Mum and Dad had faced opposition from within their own families about adopting. We unwanted babies were considered bastard children, tainted by the immoral circumstances of our conception, and yes, sometimes even within the families that took us in. Mum and Dad were good moral people who had been married for more than ten years and had been unable to conceive. They desperately wanted a family of their own but of course there was no fertility treatment available in those days. IVF was a thing of the distant future. Luckily for me, they decided that a bastard baby was the way forward for them.

And so it was against their families' wishes when they applied to adopt a child through the "National Incorporated Association for the Reclamation of Destitute Waif Children" otherwise known as Dr. Barnardo's Homes, a charity that matched available babies in their care with suitable prospective parents. After a rigorous application process, Mum and Dad were eventually accepted and put on a waiting list for a baby. While they were waiting, they were subjected to intrusive and unannounced home visits and questioned about their religious beliefs. In those days, church attendance was a prerequisite for adoption - Dr. Barnardo's being affiliated with the Church of England - and knowing the vicar of your local church on a personal basis definitely earned you bonus points. I don't know how they did it, because apart from christenings, weddings and funerals, I don't remember them ever attending church. Yet somehow they pulled it off and later I discovered they even had a letter from a local church minister recommending them as prospective parents.

Eventually Mum and Dad received a letter from Dr. Barnardo's to inform them that a suitable baby girl would soon be available, and so the long and short of it is that I became Perry Christina Coleman, daughter of Iris and Fred. They liked the name that I had already been given by my birth mother, so they decided to keep it.

Iris and Fred really knew very little about my background, or that of my adopted sister. They told us both what they knew about our pasts; in my case, that my birth mother was English and my biological father was an American and in the Air Force (I always found this fascinating). She had been much older than him, and previously divorced (doubly shameful) and that they weren't married (triply shameful). They told me I had a half-sister and half-brother from my birth mother's previous marriage, who were both much older than me. My mother had to give me up because she was a working single parent and needed to keep her job, and she couldn't do that with a new baby in tow, especially without a husband to support her. She was a secretary, back in the days when The Bosses were men and the women (who in truth ran the show) were The Secretaries. Yes, she would have lost her job if she had kept me. There was no such thing as maternity leave in those days, and mothers were expected to be married to the father of their children and to stay at home raising them. A working single mother was a real anomaly back in those days. And that really was all I knew; except that I never had the sense of being unwanted and I was loved by the parents who raised me as their own.

When I was four years old we moved from London to a village in Kent, and that was where I grew up. I am blessed to have friends from the earliest days I can remember, who have remained my friends for my whole life. I think that's what communities used to be like, and perhaps they still are; tight knit, with people forging lifelong friendships.

I have a clear memory that has stuck with me over the years, from Primary School days. I think I was five or six at the time, and I remember the day when I had told my friends at school that I was adopted. I can't remember what they said, but I do remember that they thought it was funny and they said they didn't believe me. Maybe they didn't know what it meant. But I cried because I thought it was something special to be an adopted child. In my mind's eye, I can still see a whole procession of children (in reality it was probably only six or seven at the most, my little circle, but I remember it as being a lot more, maybe a herd of about thirty) marching up the road from the playground after school, to my house, and knocking on the door. They wanted to ask Mum if I was telling the truth, and maybe find out what this adoption thing really meant. Mum had answered the door and the ones at the front very politely said, "Mrs. Coleman, (because that's how you addressed your friends' parents back then) is it true that Perry is adopted?" and bless her heart, she told them that yes, I was adopted; it was true. And she explained how they had chosen me out of all the babies at the home and brought me back with them to be their daughter. I think the little gathered crowd said a collective, "Oh!" and then in chorus, "Thank you," to my mum. They all turned tail, walked off down the driveway and went to their respective homes for tea, because it was tea time.

Being adopted didn't really matter very much then, because I thought it was a normal state of affairs. It was normal in my home, anyway. Growing up and as an older child, I sometimes wondered about it in a vague way, understanding that someone other than my mum had actually brought me into the world, but not being sure what that really meant for me, as a person. I did wonder what it was that made my birth mother give me up, and I think I questioned why it was me, and not one of her other children. Had I been less important somehow, or was it just easier to give up a new baby than one who had been around for a while? I was also curious about my name. No-one I knew had ever heard of a girl being called "Perry" and I get the same questions from almost everyone to whom I've ever been introduced, even to this day. "That's an unusual name, is it short for something?" and "Isn't that a boy's name?' and my favourite as an adult, "Oh. I was expecting a man." But the truth is, I love my name. It's not short for anything, it's also a girl's name because here I am, and if you were expecting a man, I am sure you will get over it. To this day,

I have no idea what inspired my birth mother to name me Perry Christina, but that's what she did, and I am glad she did. It's a little out of the ordinary, and I like to think that's true of me as a person, too.

I did sometimes try to imagine what my mother might have been like, and what my half-brother and half-sister were like. But more than all of that, I wondered about my American father. Did he know about me? He seemed like such a mystery, and as a child I found the very idea of him fascinating. What did he look like? Was I like him? I imagined him as tall, dark haired and blue eyed, handsome in his Air Force uniform, heroic somehow. I wondered if he had other children in America, more half-brothers or half-sisters who didn't know about me. And so it was that my thoughts and fantasies lingered in the back of my mind until I was eighteen years old, which back in those days was called your "Coming of Age". You were presented with a large symbolic silver key and your Adult Life began. With my coming of age came new autonomous rights and I decided to see what I could find out about my adoption for myself.

As a teenager I went through the usual rebellious stages and probably gave Mum and Dad some grey hairs, but apart from the normal teenage feelings of not really belonging, I was very much aware that I was different in many ways from my adoptive parents. I was discombobulated; I was just a little out of sync. I didn't look like them, I didn't sound like them, I didn't even like the same foods as them, but I loved them as my family just the same. It feels a little bit like being a square peg in a round hole and it is a strange thing to grow up as part of a family where you do not see yourself reflected in those who are closest to you. I knew that I had ideas and thoughts, likes and dislikes, ways and even mannerisms which could not been explained as "learned behaviour", but seemed to be from nature rather than nurture. It was a logical conclusion that some of these traits must have been inherited from my biological family; they were the small things that made me who I was, to some extent. I cannot say if it was this feeling of not quite fitting that piqued my interest and curiosity, but as I grew older, I wanted to know more about my background, because I wanted to know more about what made me, me.

Until 1977, St. Catherine's House in London housed the central archive for all "Vital Statistics" in England and Wales. This included records of all births, marriages and deaths almost since written records began. It's hard to grasp now in the days of digital storage, where massive amounts of information can be kept on tiny little memory sticks, disks and miniscule hard drives, but in those days everything was written out on paper and filed in alphabetical or chronological order. There were no computers, and it took entire floors in entire buildings to store all the paper records. If there were to be a fire or other disaster, the records would be lost forever, and this had happened (as I discovered later in my search) to my biological father's military records. Nowadays applications for copies of these vital documents can be made online with the pressing of a few keys or the quick touch of a finger on a screen, but when I decided to track down my original birth certificate it meant a day trip to London on the train, and a lot of patient searching through index files for the entry relating to my birth. I remember standing in a large room filled with big volumes, like a library, and leafing through so many handwritten pages, until I eventually found the original hand printed entry for my birth. I made a note of the reference number beside it and went to The Lady at the Counter to order a copy of the actual certificate. I don't think The Lady at the Counter even looked up at me, as I slid the piece of paper with the number on it through the opening in the glass. This was what she did all day; it was just another job to her, but for me this was a momentous occasion. This was the first real step I had taken in trying to find out more about me and where I came from. I wasn't sure of the information that my original birth certificate would give me, but it was a good place to start, and it didn't feel all that threatening. I wasn't really stepping out of my comfort zone; after all, it would only be a piece of paper with "something" written on it. Maybe it would help me or maybe it wouldn't.

The handwritten copy of my original Certificate of Birth arrived courtesy of Royal Mail Second Class, a few weeks later. I opened the envelope and took out the certificate. There, in a beautiful copperplate script, in black ink, was my birth mother's full name. I read it, and then I read it again, just to be sure. There she was, suddenly a real person: Edith Mary Lillian Keyes, nee Whittaker, and her last known address; The Log Cabin, Haddiscoe, Norfolk. The Log Cabin. At that time, I had no idea if that was where she still lived, if it was her home, or perhaps it was a safe haven where she had temporarily lived while she was pregnant, waiting for me to be born. It sounded romantic, in a way. And maybe even a bit American. There aren't that many log cabins in England, or there weren't in those days, anyway. You can see where my mind was going. The address did conjure up some romantic notions in my mind of how she might have lived. A warm and cosy rustic hideaway with a fireplace perhaps. And roses growing around the door. I didn't realise at this time that she had been forced into hiding herself away in a remote part of the country, lying to her family, so that she could conceal her pregnancy from everyone that knew her. My eyes went back to my birth certificate. I saw that the space reserved for my father's name was blank. How could it be that his name wasn't recorded? It made no sense, and I was desperately disappointed, but then I remembered Mum and Dad had known he was an American. Someone must have told them that, someone from Dr. Barnardo's because who else would have known? I knew I needed to find out more. That day marked the beginning of my quest to find my biological father.

Armed with my new information, I began by writing a letter to Barnardo's, as I discovered they were now called, having dropped the Dr. from their title, and the Waif references as well. Times were changing. This was still the same adoption agency that had taken me in and placed me with Mum and Dad, but they had distanced themselves from the church and moved into the modern secular world of the 1970's. I felt the answers to some of my questions had to lie with them. They would have to know more about my father, and their records were the obvious place to start. I posted my letter and was pleasantly surprised to get a prompt response inviting me to their offices for an appointment with a social worker. And so I found myself on the train from Kent, to Barkingside in Essex, to meet with a social worker called Nan. She was very pleasant, informal and friendly, and chatted easily. We had tea and digestive biscuits, and then she handed me two typewritten sheets of paper. "Read them, they will answer some questions for you," she said.

I began to read. There in the first paragraph was my birth weight. I had never known this before, and it was a revelation. I smiled. My birth mother's name, her age when she had me, thirty eight; a quick mental calculation and I realised she would by that time be around fifty six years old. She was described as a "refined person", small in stature, with light brown hair and blue eyes, and an "equable temperament". She sounded rather lovely, I thought.

Reading on, there was a brief summary of Edith's life in a nutshell; a mention of her marriage to the father of her other two children, who were as expected considerably older than me; Sandra, my half-sister had been born in 1941, and George my half-brother in 1951. Edith's husband had gone off to fight in the Second World War and had come back "a changed man". What that meant, one can only imagine. Today we have much more of an understanding of how the trauma of war can impact those caught up in it, but back then this was poorly understood. After he returned from overseas, he began drinking heavily. This had led to him "acting badly" towards her which was clearly a thinly veiled reference to domestic abuse, he had lost his job and in June 1953 she had taken the two children and left him. She moved to another part of the country entirely. This was an incredibly brave and courageous thing to do, for a woman to start a new life with two young children and without the support of a husband. She sounded like she was a strong woman. Edith filed for divorce and it was granted in December 1954. As a single parent, she needed a job to support her family. She was a resourceful and educated woman, and she got a job at the local Air Force base working as a secretary. There, she had met the man who was to be my biological father. An American Serviceman, his first name was Eugene. Finally. I had a name. Strangely, once I knew it, I felt I had known his name all along, but just mislaid it somewhere in my memory. I thought someone must have told me his name before at some point. It was an interesting name and it fitted nicely with my imagined idea of what he was like. I thought it was a slightly unusual name, and I had a feeling that he was an unusual person. Little did I know.

Reading on, I discovered that in January 1958, before I was conceived, Edith's teenage daughter Sandra discovered, horror of horrors, that she was pregnant. This must have been a blow to Edith as a single parent already supporting her two children. She would not be able to raise another child on her secretary's salary I am sure. Sandra had a steady boyfriend who she had met in school, childhood sweethearts, and a wedding was hurriedly arranged for the beginning of March. Around this time, Edith had unwisely begun an "intimate relationship" with Eugene, confiding in him about her troubles. It was apparently a short-lived dalliance because by the time Edith discovered she was pregnant, Eugene had already gone back to America. She wrote to him telling him of the baby, and he had replied offering marriage "if that was what she wanted", but she declined. Eugene was described as being "tall, with brown hair and blue eyes", and had "a pleasant personality". He sounded like a fine catch, I thought to myself. Ah well. She must have had her reasons for refusing his offer of marriage.

I realised that there was no last name for Eugene anywhere on the typed papers. No matter how hard I looked, no matter how many times I read them through, his last name was not there. I asked Nan if this was an oversight; was his name anywhere in my adoption records? She hesitated for the briefest of moments and I felt she was considering how much she could tell me. Then she answered, yes - he was identified fully in my file. I asked if I could have his name. She hesitated again, and then she told me that as my birth mother had chosen not to put his name on my birth certificate, she could not divulge that information without having Edith's permission. My heart sank a little at this news because I wasn't quite sure how Edith could be contacted all these years later to give her permission, or even if I wanted that to happen – but well, it was a start. I now knew much more than I had before.

I returned home on the train clutching my sheets of paper. I don't know what I had been expecting to find, but inside there was a part of me that felt cheated by being denied something that I felt should, by rights, be mine. Eugene's full name. He was my biological father, after all. I wanted so much to know who he was. I read the papers again, hoping for a clue, but his last name still wasn't there.

Over the next few weeks I considered whether to ask Barnardo's if they could track down Edith and ask for her permission to give me his name. Looking back now, I don't know why I had even thought they would entertain this, but I waffled back and forth on it; I wanted to know very much, but even if it were possible, finding her and asking her after all these years might present a new set of problems. She would know that I was out there looking for answers, maybe looking for her, and that I might one day come knocking on her door. I thought perhaps she might have married again. Perhaps she would not have told her new husband about me. I thought about how she might feel to be confronted with someone, me; a stranger, her child that she had given up, knocking on her door and resurrecting the secret she had buried years ago. I felt in my heart that it would not have been right to follow through, but still I wanted to know who he was. It rankled that the information was there, buried in a dusty filing cabinet in an office somewhere in Barkingside, and that strangers, people who worked there, could pull out the papers on a whim and see his name written there, and read all about him if they wanted to. Of course, no-one was going to do that. Why on earth would they? I was just being irrational, but I was hurt. Knowing who he was would somehow make him real, as it had brought Edith to life for me for the first time when I saw her name written in black and white on my birth certificate.

I thought about Edith a lot, and how hard it must have been for her when she had discovered that she was pregnant; a divorcee and working mother raising her children on her own. In the fifties, morality had a whole different meaning. Society's values of the day dictated that divorce was frowned upon; it was a rarity and notoriously difficult to obtain, especially if sought by a woman. Marriage back then was seen as a permanent state of affairs, no matter how miserable the situation was. You got married and you stayed married; you saw it through, no matter what. Divorce carried a stigma; to be divorced was to fail. A divorced woman had little chance of success in life on her own, let alone to be prosperous, and almost no hope of finding another husband, especially if she had children. Edith would have been considered "used goods". Women working outside the home had very few options when it came to jobs. The best and probably the only employment opportunities would have been in traditionally female roles such as a secretary, a librarian or perhaps at a stretch, a teacher. There was great disparity between pay for a man and pay for a woman doing a similar job. This is something we still haven't fully addressed today, but it is better than it used to be. Back then, a woman would only earn just over half of what a man would earn in a comparable role. Edith was a secretary who worked long hours for little pay and had a family to raise on her own. She would truly have been judged as second class by the society of the day. She had a lot to overcome.

Back in the fifties, having a sexual relationship outside of a marriage, either before, during or after, was completely taboo. First, Edith's teenage daughter had got pregnant and would have had no choice but to be married off as soon as possible. Then Edith herself, having unwisely become intimately involved with a co-worker, found herself expecting a baby, too. Pressure for her to give the baby up would have been immense; and let's not forget that this was truly scandalous. It wasn't hard for me to see that she had little choice but to hide the pregnancy and give her baby up. Abortion was not an available option, and for that I am truly thankful because had it been, I may never have been born.

According to my typewritten pages from Barnardo's,

Edith had been assigned a "Moral Welfare Worker". The term sounds strange, that the moral wellbeing of this poor woman was somehow at stake, but she clearly needed saving from herself before she could do herself any more damage. Of course, the alliance with the church would have dictated that this was a moral issue, and Edith was advised to save what was left of her tattered moral reputation by giving the baby up and then getting on with her life as if nothing had happened. Hard as that may have been for her, she had chosen to take that advice. I didn't blame her. It wasn't really much of a choice. It appeared that after my pregnant half-sister Sandra was married off to her boyfriend and settled into her new life, Edith had taken George, my young half-brother, away with her to a remote place where she had lived until I was born. Then she had handed me over to Barnardo's, exactly as she had been advised to do. She had then taken George and returned to her home and her secretarial job, with no-one being any the wiser.

Edith had gone right back to her old life as if nothing had happened. Like I said, she was a tough lady. She had to be. There was no real support for her or the many other women like her, and no aftercare whatsoever. How different things are today. Again, I was reminded that it felt wrong to try to track her down; I was painfully aware that this could open up old wounds. She had probably long since buried those memories, because how else could she have coped? I knew in my heart that she must have been a good person, certainly she was a determined and strong woman who had been through a tremendous amount of adversity in her life. I hoped with all my heart that she had remarried and was happy. I decided for the time being to let things rest, and I hoped that I could eventually find another route to Eugene.

There was something else to consider, too. Iris and Fred, my mum and dad. I didn't want to hurt them. They had always been very open about the fact that I was adopted, but I had a feeling that perhaps they might not understand my need to know more about my biological roots. I was afraid they would perceive this as some sort of a rejection. They had done nothing to make me think this way, but I was aware that it was potentially a source of difficulty for them. I felt this especially about my dad. I didn't feel that the time was right, so I decided to put it all to bed for a while and went on living my life.

I worked and I studied and I travelled and, gypsy that I am at heart, I eventually moved overseas, settling in Canada where I married and had two daughters of my own. Having my own children really brought it home to me just how hard it would have been to give birth to a child and then to have to give that child up. It's certainly not an easy option, and I realised it wasn't something that I could ever have done.

Throughout those years living in Canada I did not forget about Edith and Eugene. Periodically I would do some research in the hope that something would turn up. Home computers had become commonplace. The internet had arrived. Adoption was no longer considered something to be hidden. Things were more open and contact between family members of adoptees was becoming possible and was even encouraged. I signed up online with the Adoption Contact Register; a UK government service for adopted people and their birth relatives. If two biological family members were registered and both wanted to have contact, they could be matched up and their details exchanged. I hoped, but I heard nothing. I reasoned that my half-brother George may be the easiest to track down. He would probably still be George Keyes, and with luck he might still be living in the UK. I knew of course that Sandra had married and would probably have a different last name, and if Edith had remarried then she too, would be almost impossible to find. And so I began with George, looking in Norfolk where I had been born, and in Berkshire where I knew my mother had worked on the American base. Because I lived in the countryside where internet service was still tediously slow, I went to the library and pored through paper telephone directories to find addresses. I wrote letters to as many George Keyes' as I could find. I wrote, folded, sealed and took those letters to the Post office and sent them off First Class. I waited, waited some more, and I had only one reply. It was from a lady who had been married to a George Keyes. She was a widow because he had recently passed away, but he was not the George that I was seeking. She just wanted me to know that it wasn't her George that I was looking for, and to wish me luck with my search. Her letter was very touching and sensitively written; I appreciated it so very much. I've kept it.

2

MAKING HEADWAY

Fast forward about twenty years. Mum and Dad are now happily retired and living on the beautiful coast of North Cornwall in the south west of England. Cornwall is still, even today, a remote part of the country; the population swelling in the summer months with second-home owners and a huge influx of tourists, but sparsely populated during the bleak months of winter. Summer tourism fuels the economy in Cornwall, with people drawn to the beautiful beaches and rugged inland scenery. Fishing villages like Port Isaac made famous by the Doc Martin television series, Tintagel with its links to the legendary King Arthur, the wild ponies and craggy rock formations of Bodmin Moor, these are all draws for the city dwellers of England who flock to the West Country with their families during the school summer holidays. For two months every summer the tiny single-track lanes are choked with cars, the towns filled with sun tanned, flip-flop-wearing, ice-cream-eating tourists seeking out pasties and cream teas. This is summertime Cornwall.

When I was a child, as a family we had gone to Cornwall for two weeks every summer for as long as I can remember. We were lucky enough to have family who owned a holiday cottage business there, and so we had accommodation close to the beaches for a bargain price, provided we didn't want to go on "peak season" weeks. We always went for the last week of August and the first week of September every year, without fail. This was at the end of tourist season; everything was still open; the gift shops and the attractions, but the roads and beaches were so much quieter. I loved the place with its wild beauty, and so did Mum and Dad. When the time came for Dad to retire, they sold their home in expensive Sussex and bought one of the family holiday cottages in what was then much cheaper Cornwall.

The downside to living in Cornwall is that services are few and far between for the aging resident population. Mum and Dad's home was in a delightful small village on the north coast, but there was only one tiny shop which also housed the village post office, and only one bus a week into the nearest town several miles away. While they were both healthy and active this wasn't a problem. Dad drove everywhere. Mum had never learned to drive so she was completely reliant on him for getting around. Not a problem, because they went everywhere together, until he started to suffer memory loss with the onset of dementia. Then Mum, healthy as a horse all her life, had a heart attack. Suddenly with the harsh realities of age and failing health, they came face to face with the difficulties of remote country living. The nearest hospital was more than an hour's drive from their home and by then with cutbacks to what few services there had been, now there were no buses and no nearby health services whatsoever.

Mum's heart attack happened in December of 1999, the day before my birthday. I was living in British Columbia, Canada at the time, with my husband and two young daughters. There was a panicked early morning phone call from Dad; he was in pieces and didn't know what to do. Mum had suffered a serious heart attack at home and had been flown by Air Ambulance to Derriford Hospital in the neighbouring county of Devon. The drive by road to the hospital is a little over an hour and a half, but the helicopter had her there in a fraction of that time and probably saved her life. I realised very quickly that Dad wasn't able to cope. They had hidden his advancing dementia well, but suddenly it was obvious, and I was too far away to be of any immediate help. My adopted sister was living in Plymouth where Mum was in hospital, but she didn't drive either and wasn't able to step in in a meaningful way to help Dad. Fortunately Mum made a spectacular recovery, but the seed was sown in my mind that I needed to be closer; it was inevitable that they would need help and support if not now, then certainly in the near future. So in 2002 we sold our home in Canada, packed up lock stock and barrel and relocated to England to make it our home; if not permanently then certainly for the foreseeable future.

We settled in Devon, not so close as to be on Mum and Dad's doorstep, but close enough to be able to be there when they needed help, and to visit them often. My daughters were then aged six and seven and were soon settled into school in the village where were living. I, thinking I needed a job that was secure and well paid (because England was an expensive place to live at that time compared to Canada) had been lucky enough to be accepted into the local police force as a trainee. It was to become my career for the next ten years. And so we started our new life.

With my return to England came a renewed interest in my adoption quest. It had never really left me, always sitting there in the back of my mind but I had been busy having children of my own and living my life in Canada for fifteen years. During my absence from England, the Data Protection Act of 1998 had been passed into law. This Act governed the storage and use of personal information held on people by what is termed an Organisation. Barnardo's fit the criteria and now this Act gave me the legal right to find out what information was held about me, and to be entitled to a copy of that information. It seemed to me that if Eugene's full name was recorded in my adoption file at Barnardo's, I was now legally entitled not only to see it, but also to have a copy of it. I applied in writing to Barnardo's straight away. As per their legal requirement, I received a response from Barnardo's within the allowed forty days. I was informed that my inquiry had been received; I was on a waiting list and my request would be processed in due course. I was told this could take up to a year, but I didn't care. I had waited a long time already and waiting a little longer didn't matter. I was hopeful I could finally get somewhere.

I filled in the time by researching at the local library and online at home with what information I already had. I tried to find out if Edith were still alive by checking death records, and although I was doubtful that she would be as she would have been well into her eighties by then, I found I couldn't confirm that she was dead. I searched for Eugene and discovered to my surprise that this was a relatively common first name in America. Of course, without any details other than his first name and the fact that he was an American serviceman based in the UK during a particular timeframe, it was pure fantasy to think that I might actually be able to find him, but I tried anyway.

Finally, after several weeks I received a letter from Making Connections. This is a support service provided by Barnardo's for people like me, and the letter said that my case was being handled by one of their social workers. It was confirmed that I would be given access to my adoption records. As was suggested in the letter I received, I made called and made an appointment to meet with Sue, my designated social worker.

I was experiencing déjà vu on the train journey to

Barkingside on the way to my appointment with Sue. This time I hoped I would be getting some concrete information; all of it, not just another person's interpretation of part of my records on two typed sheets of paper. I was nervous but excited at the prospect of seeing and reading my actual adoption file.

I was very glad of the ten minute walk from the London Underground station at Barkingside to Barnardo's Head Office. I really needed the air after the four hour long train journey from Devon, followed by thirty minutes travelling on the stuffy "Tube". I walked through the Barnardo's complex, following the directions on a map I had been given, and into the main reception area. After I had checked in for my appointment, Sue came out to greet me. She offered me coffee (not tea this time), and then walked with me into a small office. She had a large file folder with her, which I presumed contained my adoption records. She then explained that she would go through the papers with me in roughly chronological order, answer any questions I had along the way and then leave for a few minutes to give me time to read some more and gather my thoughts. She took a large stack of papers out of the file folder and placed them on the table. The pile of papers was about two inches thick, with yellow "Post-It's" stuck in between some of the pages. These, she explained, were items she considered to be of particular importance. "There's a lot of information there," she said, "I just picked out some of the more important things along the way."

She passed me the first two sheets of paper. This was the same summary Nan had handed to me all those years ago. "I expect this is what they gave you when you came before," she said. I nodded. I noticed that it was a poor copy and quite difficult to read the small and blurry type. She explained, "It's been copied from microfiche records. The original papers were destroyed years ago." I read the summary again, although I knew it mostly by heart.

Then Sue passed me the next sheet. It was stamped in red, "STRICTLY CONFIDENTIAL', with the words written underneath, "TO BE KEPT UNDER LOCK AND KEY." I began to read. My name was at the top, Perry Christina Keyes, along with my date of birth and the date of my admission to Barnardo's. I skim-read down the sheet of paper: my mother's full name, her age, her income and address. And then, there it was in black and white: *"Father (putative): Eugene Gallagher (22) American; was a Serviceman; health good."* This was followed by a "General Delivery" address in North Carolina, USA. I remember feeling very emotional. Sue had a large box of tissues and she handed me one. All those years of wondering who he was and finally here was his name. He was real at last. I was elated.

I realised with a shock that he had only been twenty two years old, and Edith was a full sixteen years older than he was. This would have been an absolute scandal in its day. Of course, since he was that much younger, there would be a good chance he was still alive. This filled me with hope.

Reading on, there was a comprehensive account of Edith's life prior to her meeting Eugene. It was obvious that she was a victim of domestic abuse at the hands of her ex-husband, and that she had fled in fear with the children from Liverpool to Berkshire to begin a new life. The file recounted a relationship she had with another American serviceman (his name redacted); this man had wanted to marry her, but she had declined citing that her daughter Sandra did not want to go to live in America and she therefore could not leave. Edith had lost touch with this man after he returned to the United States. I asked Sue why his name was redacted, and she explained that because this was "third party information" which did not relate directly to me, it was not disclosable. I wondered if he was somehow the elusive "Perry" connection.

Eugene was a friend of this man, and Edith had sought his counsel after Sandra was found to be pregnant. They had then "become intimate", and Edith later found she also was pregnant. Reading on, that Edith had taken her young son George with her to Norfolk for several months to hide her pregnancy and have her baby. *"The mother has not told any of her relatives about her lapse,"* I read. I felt this was so sad; she could not confide in her family or really anyone about her situation. I could not help a wry smile though at the description of the events leading to my conception as a "lapse" by the otherwise woman of good character.

Continuing to read, my heart was touched by the kindness of the complete strangers who owned the caravan in Norfolk, where it has been arranged my birth mother and George would be staying. Edith's boss, and the only person in whom she had confided, had made the arrangements. The owner of the small caravan, Mrs. Thurston, knowing that my mother was suffering financial hardship, refused to take any rent from her. She had also looked after George for the time that my birth mother was "in confinement" at the hospital. I found this profoundly moving. Then, with tears in my eyes I read that, after being discharged from hospital nine days after my birth, Edith had left me in the care of Mr. and Mrs. Thurston and immediately returned to Berkshire with George. Who were these wonderful people who had taken in a stranger's baby, refusing any payment and really had no good reason for doing any of that, except out of the kindness of their hearts?

As I continued reading through the papers, I realised that they had looked after me not just for a few days, but for several weeks. And besides, Mrs. Thurston had negotiated on my mother's behalf with the Moral Welfare Worker and

Barnardo's and had then herself delivered me safely into the hands of the "Travelling Matron" in late January 1959. These were special people indeed: I resolved to try to find them, so that I could thank them from the bottom of my heart for what they did for me and for my birth mother, who they had barely really known.

I had not been expecting to see copies of handwritten notes and letters that my birth mother had sent to Barnardo's. This took my breath away. Edith had sent money for my keep while I was there, although it was clear she could barely afford to. Some payments were late and there were handwritten apologetic notes. Every payment she had made had been accompanied by a completed and signed payment slip. In her elaborate, curly-yet-neat handwriting, in one note she asks for a Barnardo's collection box to put in her office at work (I was especially touched by this); in another note she enquires whether all is well with the adoption process, apparently concerned that I "may have been found in some way or other not suitable". It seems I had been born with a club foot which was a physical defect and any baby less than perfect would not be put up as available for adoption. Happily, the condition was mild and was resolved with a leg brace which I wore for some months. I read these notes in nothing short of wonderment; it was a tiny glimpse into my birth mother's thoughts at the time and gave me a hint of the kind of woman she was.

Later in the file there was correspondence between Barnardo's and my mum and dad as they were told that a "suitable baby" had been found. This touched my heart; I realised perhaps for the first time how important it had been to them to have the chance for a family of their own. There was a letter in my dad's handwriting, from the days when people wrote their own letters with paper and pen, and their excitement at the prospect of finding a baby girl was palpable. By the time I had got my appointment with Making Connections, Dad had passed away and this brought thoughts of him back to me with a rush. Mum and Dad had fostered me at first. Dad had been in the hospital with tuberculosis for several months, and he had to be free and clear of the illness before they could bring me home. Everyone seemed to be unsure whether my birth mother would go through with the adoption process and this had been a difficult time for them, as I could have been taken back at any time. Finally, well over a year later the adoption was completed. It was official, I was stamped "ADOPTED" on 30th March 1960. The Judge's gavel had fallen, and the signed paperwork was ordered to be sealed. That is, until the Data Protection Act changed everything for adoptees like me.

After Sue had left the room as she had said she would, I was reading through one of the early reports in the file by the Moral Welfare Worker. She had visited my birth mother at the caravan in Norfolk prior to my birth, so clearly Edith had made the decision to place me with Barnardo's for adoption some months before I was born. Suddenly a sentence leapt out at me from that report. Following a brief physical description of my birth mother was typed the following: *"The same description applies to the put. father, except that he is 6' in ht. "A photograph of the man is attached."* A photograph of Eugene? There was a photograph of Eugene? I leafed through the file papers but there was no photograph that I could see.

Sue came back into the room and sat down. She picked up the file from which she had taken the papers and took out some black and white photographs. "These were in your file," she explained, handing me the first one. I recognised it immediately. It was a photograph I had seen before, of me as a young child perhaps three years old. It was taken by my dad and I realised he must have sent a copy to Barnardo's for some reason, perhaps when they had adopted their second child, my sister. The second photograph was a postcard showing St. Christopher's, the Barnardo's home where I had been placed. It was a beautiful Victorian villa in a park-like setting. There were some old-fashioned prams on the lawn and children playing. I do have memories of that place, although I have been told that cannot be so, as I was only a baby when I was there. But I can recall a large and airy room with doors opening out onto the lawn. There were lines of cots in the room. When I looked at the postcard, I could see those doors at the bottom left of the building. It felt quite surreal. I also have distinct memories of a park nearby with large elaborate iron gates, and a lake with a curved shore. I later found out that for a while before they were able to "board me out", Mum and Dad would visit me weekly at St. Christopher's and take me for walks to the park across Pembury Road, pushing me in my pram. "The house was sold many years ago," Sue said, "it's no longer a children's home."

She handed me the final photograph. "This was in your file as well," she explained, "We don't know whether it was put there by accident. It doesn't seem to belong in there." I looked at the photograph. It was a snapshot of three men standing in a casual relaxed pose outside a building with metal-framed windows. The two men to the left looked younger than the man on the right. The young man on the far left had his hands in his pockets and was smiling widely. He was tall, with dark hair. Above his head, on the white border of the photograph was a cross marked in blue ink, and a tiny blue arrow pointing down to him. I instantly thought, "*A photograph of the man is attached.*" Could this really be a photograph of Eugene?

I said to Sue, "It says in the file that there's a photograph of my father." Sue looked surprised, so I showed her where it was written in the Moral Welfare Worker's report. Sue said she very much doubted that would be the case; it would have been highly unusual for a photograph of a birth parent to be placed in an adoption file. I asked her if I could have the photograph anyway, and she agreed. I think I already knew in my heart that it was him; I could hardly believe that not only had I found out his name, but I also may now know what he looked like. Later, that photograph was to prove invaluable when I finally tracked down Eugene's family.

My head was spinning when I got back to the railway station to begin the train ride home to Devon. I had stopped for a bite to eat in a pub on the way to the station, but now my stomach was aching. I felt physically sick. I didn't know whether it was what I had eaten, or the emotion of the day taking its toll on me. I couldn't sit; I felt nauseous and spent the entire train journey walking between the train carriages.

When I eventually arrived at home, exhausted but beyond sleep, I went straight upstairs to the office and logged on to the computer. I typed 'Eugene Gallagher, North Carolina' into the search bar and hit Enter. Up on the screen instantly came a photograph of a smiling middle-aged man and woman. It was a wedding photograph dated 2004. The bride, the smiling woman, was a daughter of the Late Eugene Rexton Gallagher of Red Springs, North Carolina. Looking at her face I knew right away that we were related. There could not be any doubt. Her mouth and eyes were so similar to mine. I cannot describe how I felt. This was truly an incredible moment. I had never before in my life seen another person who looked like so much like me. That night when I finally went to bed, I was thinking that I may have found a sister. After all she was a daughter of Eugene Gallagher, and that was my biological father's name. I had however acknowledged the word "late" in front of his name and realised that if she were indeed my sister, that he must be dead.

3

All Aboard the Rollercoaster

Thank goodness for the internet; what an amazing source of information. The woman in the photograph was called Jolene. It suited her. She was Southern, sassy and blonde, standing confidently with her man in front of the camera on her wedding day. She looked about the same age as me. The photo had been published in the local newspaper, and I hoped she still lived in the same town. Half an hour of researching census records later, I knew that she did, and her address was easily found. I could not believe how quickly I had located her. I still had to confirm she was in fact related to me, but in my heart I already knew. We looked too similar for it to be a coincidence.

The next day I bought a subscription to an ancestry website, and very quickly discovered that Jolene was the youngest of eight children, five girls and three boys. The oldest was a girl, Belle, born in 1935; Jolene was born in 1953 and was just five years older than me. The remaining six were born at regular intervals in between Belle and Jolene. Their father had indeed been Eugene Gallagher, his full name Eugene Rexton Gallagher, Senior. He was not my father; he was my paternal grandfather and Jolene was not my sister, she was my aunt. Her oldest brother was my father. In keeping with tradition, the oldest son was often given the name of the father, and so my father was Eugene Rexton

Gallagher, Junior. He was born in 1937. This was the young American serviceman who had come to England and met my birth mother, Edith. This was exciting news, and I was relieved because he was not the Late Eugene Rexton Gallagher. At that moment, I believed he was still living.

Hardly believing that things could be moving so quickly after taking so long to get to this point, I took a moment and pondered over how best to make the initial contact with Jolene. I had her telephone number, but I thought a phone call might be too much, too soon, and anyway she could hang up. I thought about how I might feel if a stranger phoned me out of the blue, claiming to be a hitherto unknown close relative. Firstly I'd be suspicious, and I quite possibly wouldn't believe it. I might well hang up. I decided that writing a short letter explaining what I had discovered, and who I was, and then asking if she would mind having contact with me would be the best approach. I felt that handwritten would be best and seem more personal. She could see I was a real person then, rather than an anonymous "somebody" typing words on a keyboard and printing off an impersonal sheet of copy paper. It's strange because I don't suppose anyone handwrites letters at all today, but even just a few short years ago it was still considered to be the way to communicate with a personal touch.

I actually had to go out and buy a pad of writing paper because I had none in the house. I didn't write a lot of letters. When I got back home, I sat down and carefully composed my letter to Jolene, feeling a bit like I was reaching out blind and not knowing what I would find. I made several attempts and created a bin full of failed efforts before I was happy with what I had written. I sealed the finished letter into a blue Airmail envelope. I knew how important this letter was. This was the first contact with anyone who knew my biological father. I wondered how Jolene would feel when she read the letter and whether she would respond. I really hoped she would. I had it in my heart that it was right somehow to contact her first. I said a quick prayer that she would receive the letter safely and have an open heart to receive what I had to say, and then I walked to the post office and mailed the letter.

With the letter safely on its way in the hands of the Royal Mail, I continued with my research on the ancestry site hopeful that Eugene was still alive and that I would be able to locate him. Within a few hours my hopes were dashed when I discovered the record of his death. It was basic, just his name, his social security number, his date of birth and date of death. He had died at home in Thomasville, North Carolina on New Year's Eve 1978. I thought perhaps he may have had a heart attack because he had been so young, only forty one at the time of his death. This was such a rollercoaster of emotions; I did cry for the father I had never met, sad that I would never have that chance. Growing up, knowing that he was younger than Edith, I had always assumed he would still be living, and I had hoped one day to meet him. I felt a strange affinity with him, and the American side of my birth family. I cannot explain why, but it was important for me to find out more about him – Eugene, the person - from his surviving brothers and sisters.

I had given Jolene my email address in the letter, and a week or so after I had sent it off on a wing and a prayer in the mail, there was a response from her sitting in my email in-box. It was headed simply, "Hello". This was my first direct contact with anyone from my birth family. I clicked on the Open button. Her message was quite short, but the font was large, bold and purple. I would soon learn that this was signature Jolene. Outgoing, direct and to the point, everything about her big and bold, no small talk. I read the message.

Jolene referred to her brother using his middle name of Rexton rather than his first name of Eugene. She said she had no idea what he had been up to in 1958 as she had only been five years old. But what caught my attention right away were the words, "We know Rexton had a little girl in England who hasn't been seen since she was three or four years old." She apologised for not being able to help me more, then she wished me luck with finding answers.

I gave this some careful thought and wondered about this little girl in England. I was a bit shocked because I felt it couldn't possibly be me. I had been given up by my mother for adoption well before I was a year old, and finally adopted in early 1960, long before I was two years old. Did this mean I might have another half-sister out there somewhere? I emailed Jolene and thanked her for her reply. I asked her if she could let me know if she found out anything more from her siblings. She responded almost straight away; I had the feeling from the way she wrote that she was a friendly and open person, but her words were carefully guarded, protective and almost defensive about her family. Understandable in the circumstances, I thought. She was quite clear that she could not and would not give me information about her sisters or her one surviving brother, but she was happy to talk about herself. She said they had a rule that they didn't speak about each other without the other's permission. Later the meaning behind her words came to make perfect sense but at the time I didn't appreciate what lay behind them. I was still reaching out blindly, wondering what – or who - I would find next.

After we had exchanged a few conversational emails, Jolene agreed to talk to me about Eugene, but she was concerned to confirm that the Eugene Gallagher I had contacted her about was in fact her brother, and not some other person of the same name. Apparently, there were more

Eugene Gallaghers in North Carolina than I could have known or imagined. It had seemed like such an unusual name to me, but she was right. When I checked, there definitely were others. Cue the photograph in my adoption file; I could settle this one way or the other and I decided to send her a copy to see if the smiling man on the left side of the picture was, in fact, Eugene Rexton Gallagher, brother of Jolene. I scanned the photograph, attached it to my email message and pressed the send button, holding my breath. The response to that photograph was incredible. At first, a short message back from Jolene to say she would know her brother's sweet face anywhere; yes, it was him, he was Eugene Gallagher, my biological father. And now suddenly it became real to me; he was no longer just a smiling man in a photograph, he was a person with a real life and a history. This gave me real hope that I could get to know Eugene the man, my father, through his surviving family.

After this revelation, I received another email almost straight away from one of Jolene's older sisters, Roseanne. It was written all in upper case; short, sharp sentences that spoke loudly of the pain of losing of her brother. The hurt simply radiated off the screen as I read her message.

"HE SHOULD NOT HAVE DIED…"

The words hit me hard; sowing the seed in my mind for the first time that perhaps it had not been a natural death as I had assumed.

"PLEASE, NO GAMES", she said, "THIS IS A HURTING PART OF MY LIFE."

I wrote back straight away. No, no games, I told her. I don't play games with people's lives. I told her about myself, my family and what little I knew of my birth mother. I asked her how Eugene had died. I had expected a quick response, like I had from Jolene, but the minutes passed by and she didn't reply. I didn't hear back from Roseanne for quite a while.

But with Jolene, suddenly everything was happening at once. Fast and furious over the next few days there were flurries of exchanged emails and family photographs. We were like two little children excited by a newfound friendship. She spliced a photo I had sent her of me, alongside a photo of her at about the same age. "Do we look like kinfolk? Do we!!!!" she said. Kinfolk, such a cool word, and so American. We were kin. She sent me a school photograph of herself as a small child. We looked so similar, there was no doubting we were closely related; we could actually have passed for sisters. This was an exciting and heady time for me; for the first time in my life seeing what my blood relatives looked like – my grandparents, my aunts, my uncles. The Gallaghers on my grandfather's side, the Russells on my grandmother's. Like Jolene, I favoured the Russell side of the family in colouring, body type and probably personality, too.

Jolene told me that Eugene had three other daughters and had been married to a woman called Louisa; she thought he had adopted the oldest child, but the other two were his natural children. They had not been seen or heard from since Eugene had died in 1978. This was bitter-sweet, on one hand it was great news – I had more half-sisters out there - but no-one knew where they were. This would mean a lot more digging. I was puzzled by how and why they had all lost touch. It didn't seem to make much sense. And who was the little girl Jolene had referred to in her first message to me? Not one of them, she had said she had thought it must be me. More research was definitely needed.

When Roseanne finally replied to my email about a week later, there were more revelations. She told me that Eugene had known he had a daughter in England; he had travelled back after leaving the service and met with the child's mother after I was born, and had then returned to America with two photographs, one of him with (who Roseanne presumed to be) Edith, and the other of them both with a little girl, presumed to be me. The photographs had been given to my grandmother and put in the family photo album. Roseanne promised to try to find them. She thought her older sister Belle had them somewhere. This was intriguing.

Roseanne said that Edith had also been to Eugene's house in North Carolina in 1962 or 1963, and Roseanne recalled him going to pick her up once after that from Raleigh-Durham airport, she thought in 1974. She had argued with him, knowing that he was still involved on some level with this other woman from England whilst being married to Louisa. Roseanne said she and Louisa were very close, like sisters. I wondered what on earth Edith would be doing visiting him in America, and how long they had carried on seeing each other after I was born. This was a strange development.

I was very surprised that Eugene had travelled back to England to see this daughter of his, and I was puzzled by it. too. I was sure it could not be me. I did not understand how he would have been able to have a photograph taken with me – I had been given up for adoption as a baby and to the best of my knowledge I would not have had any further contact with my birth mother, let alone a visit from my biological father. Had Edith ever made any attempts to rekindle contact with me, Barnardo's would have never allowed the adoption to continue. It had been my mum and dad's greatest fear. So who was this little girl?

At the time of writing, the mystery of those photographs in the Gallagher family album remains. The album is not with Belle, but in the hands of another aunt who wishes to have no contact with me. She is a very private person, and at the centre of what I would later come to call "the sisterhood", a protective bond between some of my aunts formed in childhood for reasons that would later become clear. Roseanne, although friendly, seemed very reluctant to ask her sister for the photographs, saying that she was stubborn and strong-minded. She alluded to "family dysfunction" but did not elaborate. I didn't want to ask her about that, as I felt it didn't directly concern me, but I did want to know about those photos.

I thought I'd try contacting this other sister myself. I had her email address from her being copied into messages that Roseanne and Jolene had sent me, so I knew they had told her about me. In my naivety I thought she might be open to sharing whatever she could about Eugene, but at first, she simply ignored my attempts to contact her. Ever the optimist, I did not take that as necessarily negative, but later she wrote a letter to another family member who shared it with me, which went some way towards explaining her actions. In that letter she said she did not want "strangers" going through her parents' personal things; doubtless a reference to the family photograph albums. She doesn't see me as part of the family, and I have no choice but to accept that. Sue, the social worker at Barnardo's, had told me that not everyone will necessarily welcome a new member of the family, and I should expect that this may happen. My aunt is not alone in this and doubtless she has her reasons. I am still hopeful that she will one day change her mind, as this is a mystery I would like to solve. It may be that there is yet another sister for me to find out there.

Roseanne told me more about my father. He was a tall, upstanding man who strutted when he walked. He was proud and hard-working; he didn't sit still; he was always busy. I could relate to that. Like father, like daughter, I thought. She described him as her hero and she clearly adored him. She especially had been devastated by his early death. Her words,

"He should not have died…" made me wonder again what had happened to him. If he had died of natural causes, for example a heart attack then yes, it would have been sudden and unexpected. But I felt there was something more to this, and sure enough the very next message I had from Roseanne dropped like a bombshell into my inbox. It started with this sentence,

"My brother was shot in the back by his wife and died instantly."

I could not have prepared myself for how much those words would hurt. At the outset, before I had started my search, I had made a conscious decision to take whatever I found as it was, good or bad. Not to back away or hide from the truth because it was uncomfortable or even painful, or not what I wanted to hear. But I had never expected this.

Louisa had killed him, and not just killed him in a horrible yet tragic accident, she had shot him in the back. This was surely murder. It was awful, and I was shocked. Of all things, this had not been something I had seen coming. Suddenly I had a whole new perspective and a lot more questions. What had happened? Why had she shot him? Was it because of Edith? Did Louisa go to prison? Was she still alive? What happened to the children? This had really gotten to me and I cried for a long time.

Roseanne told me about Louisa and Eugene. They had been married for fifteen years, and it was a stormy relationship. He was a difficult man and "liked his women", but for the last four years of his life he had been a Christian. He had been born again, and this had changed him and their marriage for the better. He had given his life to God and was an active member of the church. Roseanne told me that she, too, was now a believer, as were many other members of her family. The belief is that they will one day be reunited with their loved ones, including Eugene, in Heaven. But he should not have died so soon.

I honestly didn't know how to process the news Roseanne had given me, but I felt I could understand a little more of her pain. Louisa had been her best friend and had taken the life of her brother. I could now see why there had been no contact with Eugene's other daughters, although of course they could not possibly be held to blame. Roseanne explained that the family hadn't wanted the girls to have to choose sides. It made sense on some level, but I wondered how anyone could turn their back on those girls after they had lost their father.

Roseanne found a photograph of Eugene's oldest daughters and sent it to me. Their names were Carla and Jean. Being Eugene and Louisa's daughter, Jean was my natural half-sister. I wondered if he had named her Jean as a nod to the tradition of naming your child after yourself. Usually it was the first son, as it had been for Eugene himself, but it wasn't uncommon to name your oldest daughter after yourself, either. Jean after all is the feminine version of the male name Gene. Interesting. Carla was Louisa's daughter, but her father was another man. She had been raised as Eugene's after he married her mother. Eugene and Louisa also had another younger daughter, Carrie, who was not in the photograph, and had probably not been born when that photo was taken. Jean and Carla, two sweet little blonde girls, smiling, dressed in their Sunday best. It was a beautiful photograph. Carrie was dark I was told; a little thing, intense. I wondered what they would look like today. Now I had more half-sisters to find as well, but first I needed to find out whether Edith was still alive.

4

English Connections

I went back to my computer and began researching Edith's family. With their full names in my adoption records I went looking for my half-siblings Sandra and George. It was fortunate that Sandra had never moved from the area where she had grown up, and I located her address fairly quickly, as well as that of her daughter, coincidentally also called Jean, who was my niece. Two Jeans, one on each side of the family. What were the chances? In fact, "English Jean" as I will call her, to differentiate from "American Jean" my half-sister, was just a few months older than me. Born in July of 1958, English Jean was the baby that Sandra had been expecting when Edith began her dalliance with Eugene. English Jean and I were just months apart in age.

As it had worked so well before with Jolene in America, I decided to write to both Sandra and Jean, this time giving my telephone number as well as my email address. They could phone me if they wanted, or they could write or email me. Whichever was preferable for them. It was Jean who made the first move; she telephoned me. Her voice was soft, but I felt there was an edge to it. Caution, perhaps. She certainly sounded matter-of-fact and to the point; perhaps testing the waters ahead of her mother. She said, "I think you know you've got the right person." She told me her mother was shocked and nervous. Sandra wanted to speak to me, but she wasn't ready to, not yet. She needed some time. I said, "Of course she does, only when she's ready – there's no rush." Then I heard the click and dial tone after she had said her piece. I put the handset down, wondering what would happen next.

I must have passed the initial test from Jean, because within ten minutes Sandra called me. When she spoke, I noticed she had a faintly rolling lilt to her accent which I subconsciously noted; it was unfamiliar to my ear. She told me straight away that Edith was still alive. My heart leapt; I had never dared to hope for this, especially after finding out that Eugene was dead. Sandra said, "I won't tell you exactly where she is. I will only tell you this much, she is in a nursing home in America. She's eighty nine years old." I did not fully understand the significance of what she said at the time, but with those words she had firmly laid down the law. She had drawn her line clearly in the sand at the very outset. She was in control.

Sandra told me that although she had been shocked to get my letter as she had no idea about me, it had reminded her of a seed planted in her mind years before. It was something that her younger brother George had mentioned after he and their mother had returned from a long stay in Norfolk. Edith had told the family she was having a nervous breakdown and needed to get away for a rest. When she and George returned several months later, there had been a family function of some kind and George who was just a little boy, made a flippant remark about ladies getting fat when they were having babies. The idea that George would even know such a thing was thought to be ridiculous at the time; but Sandra had noted this and wondered just how George could have come up with this notion. How well my mother had hidden my existence from her family, I thought. Her story was accepted without question at the time, and little George was promptly ushered out of the room before he could say anything else.

Sandra told me that Edith had married another American serviceman from the base and had gone to live in America with him in 1961, taking George with her. Her new husband Roy was a good provider. Sandra explained it this way: "She had his chequebook, and he had a housekeeper," she said, "That's all she married him for. She never loved him, she never loved anyone." Such bitterness in her words and tone, and I found myself wondering what kind of woman my birth mother had really been. As if reading my mind, she answered the question for me. "She was hard, cruel. She hated children." Already I was thinking how lucky I might have been to have been given up at birth, but this sat uncomfortably alongside the handwritten messages from Edith in my adoption file, and the image of the woman who had taken her children and fled from her violent husband.

Edith's husband Roy was a Master Sergeant in the American Air Force, committed to his job, and committed to young George who he loved as his own child. The family had lived in Nebraska for many years. George was still living there but he had a lot of "problems", according to Sandra. No wonder I hadn't been able to find him in England. He had been legally adopted by Roy after the marriage and had taken his last name – and he had been in America all along.

George was currently in rehab. He was an alcoholic. Stunned by this incredible amount of information in my first contact with Sandra, I took a deep breath or two. Still buoyed by the possibility of perhaps being able to meet Edith despite Sandra's apparent reticence, I asked her, "How is she? How's her health?" Sandra replied, "She's a bit senile now. She's frail." And then straight away she added "You wouldn't like her. She's not a nice person." She told me that she and her mother had never really got on at all until the last few years, and that Edith had been at best unkind to her, at worst hateful. She said, "Every year I go out to America to see her and I always say she won't make me cry. But she always does."

Sandra said, "She wanted nothing to do with Jean when she was born, she hates little girls," And then she added quietly, "Now I think I know why." I didn't know what to say, so I said nothing. Then, with a new and stronger tone in her voice, "Don't ask me where she is, I will never let you see her or talk to her. I need to protect her from this," she said. This made no sense at all to me – in one breath Sandra was describing a stern, hard, hateful woman incapable of having a close relationship with her own children, or anyone, and in the next saying that she wanted to protect her. In a way my heart went out to Sandra; I wondered if it was her that needed protecting, or at least the fragile bond that she seemed to have only recently established with her mother. It seemed as if Sandra had grown up desperate for her mother's love and had only found something approaching approval from her in the last few years. Perhaps she thought I would get in the way. But I had come this far, so I asked her again, "Will you at least tell me where she is?" She was silent for a moment, and then she said, "She's in Las Vegas. It's a big enough place that you won't find her. And I won't help you, it won't be my doing."

Sandra was happy to give me a telephone number for George, although she warned me that it might be difficult to talk to him; this was a communal telephone for the secure rehab unit where he had been living for the past six months. I asked her where in Nebraska he was, and she bluntly said, "I don't know that." I didn't believe that for a moment. And anyway, I could find that out very easily from the area code. She told me George had lost all his money and had finally hit rock bottom. He had a daughter from his first marriage,

Emma, who had been trying to support him. George's marriage had ended in divorce; much later he had remarried, but his second wife had sadly passed away. Although his circumstances seemed far from cheerful, Sandra described George as a "happy drunk"; always the life and soul of the party, who had not realised he had a real problem with drink until it was too late. Emma had her problems, too but was now firmly back on the straight and narrow. We said our goodbyes, and I hung up the phone. So ended our first conversation, with a promise to stay in touch and maybe meet in person when everyone was ready for it.

Reflecting on the conversation, which I did for quite a while, I realised that Sandra had not told me George's last name. Obviously, he was no longer George Keyes, as he had taken Roy's name. I realised Sandra had carefully protected her mother's identity so that I wouldn't have any leads in tracing her. She had already given this quite a lot of thought. In retrospect it is obvious she had determined even before our first conversation that she would do everything in her power to prevent me from contacting Edith. But I felt sure that after she had met me, she would realise I was no threat to the relationship she had established with her mother.

I telephoned George. I was nervous. I had wondered what I would say to this man who was my half -brother, who I had never met and didn't know. In preparation, I had made notes before I made the call, in case I got tongue-tied or ran out of words to say. I dialled the number. The area code was Omaha, Nebraska. A man answered the phone, and I simply asked for George. "George? George who?" came the response. "I don't know his last name." I said, feeling stupid, but I heard the person at the other end shout over the background hubbub of voices for George to come to the phone. There was a lot of loud talking going on in the background. Then I heard a soft voice say, "Hello?" He had an American accent. I don't know why that surprised me. Well, why wouldn't he? I introduced myself as Perry from England and he said straight away that Sandra had contacted him and told him about me. I could still hear voices talking excitedly all around him. It sounded as if he was constantly being pestered by other people; raised voices and commotion. It sounded chaotic. He stopped talking at one point, telling me to hold on. "Look, this is my sister on the phone. I just found out I have a sister. Can you give me a break?" There was silence for a few minutes after that.

Not surprisingly, it was a slightly awkward and rather stilted conversation. George had clearly been primed by Sandra not to say anything about our mother, and I believe from how he responded to my questions that although he went along with this, he felt badly about it. He was apologetic, "Sandra has always had her problems with Mother, but I think she brought most of it upon herself." I wondered what he meant by that. "She doesn't want you to know where she is, and I can sort of understand that. I have to respect that," he said. I didn't ask him to elaborate. This already seemed like a family with problems enough, and I didn't want to make things worse.

George chose his words carefully about our mother. He said, "She's a very strict person, very moral. She has her ways, and nothing can move her from them." He told me how he had taken his soon-to-be second wife to meet her and his stepfather Roy. They had driven for hours to get there; Roy and Edith were by then living in Texas, having moved there from Nebraska. When they finally arrived, Edith had taken the moral high ground and refused to allow George and his fiancée to sleep in the same room. Tired from their journey and upset by her attitude, they had left and got a hotel room. He laughed at the memory though, "It's seems so funny now. That was what she was like, moral: that's why this is all so unbelievable," he said. "Who would have thought she could have done this?" Who indeed? It seemed to me that she had built her wall very carefully. No-one would ever suspect that such a strongly principled person could ever have had a baby out of wedlock. It would be unthinkable. If anyone had somehow found out, they would never have believed it of her.

George remembered the long stay at the caravan with his mother before I was born. He told me that he recalled playing in some old railway carriages on the property, and he went to school, but he had no idea where it was, or who the people were who had been so kind to them. But they had been kind, he remembered that. He hadn't known that his mother had gone into hospital and had a baby, but he did remember some talk of this later with his sister Sandra, and he remembered holding a baby and someone telling him to be careful not to drop her. He was just a little boy at the time. I asked him if he had an email address so that I could send him some photographs; he said he didn't have a computer but that I could send them to Emma. Sandra would have her email address; I should ask her for it. Frankly, I wasn't sure she'd give it to me. She seemed to have a lot to hide and was preparing the way ahead of me so that I would only find out as little as possible.

I was glad I had phoned George, but I was becoming all too aware that Sandra had been closing and locking the doors ahead of me as she went. George and I said goodbye. I had the feeling that this was something I really didn't need to bother George with. He was my brother and maybe one day the time would be right, but there were too many things standing in the way of us establishing a relationship. Not least, I felt, my new-found half-sister Sandra.

5

Mixed Messages

I took flowers when I went to meet Sandra a few weeks later. It was three long hours of motorway driving during which I had lots of time to contemplate what she would be like in person. I was nervous. I had gotten very mixed signals from her during our telephone conversations. She said she wanted to meet me and get to know me, but I was apprehensive and wondered how it would be possible to develop any meaningful relationship with her if she were going to put roadblocks in the way of me finding Edith. But this was too soon to be thinking of those things. We had never even met. I reminded myself it was one small step at a time. I wanted her to see that I was a good person, and that I didn't intend to threaten what I felt was her fragile relationship with her mother. She was my half-sister after all, and the first one of my birth family that I was going to see in the flesh.

I got to the road where she lived. These were cookie-cutter neat brick terraced houses, probably built in the 1950's. I parked my car and got out. Sandra's was the house in the middle with the concrete front yard and a simply amazing display of flowers in containers, pots and hanging baskets. This was a picture of low maintenance living; easy care uPVC double glazed windows and no lawn to mow, just the containers of flowers to water. It was so very English, I thought. Like Mum and Dad's bungalow in Cornwall, something about the way it looked spoke of an older generation. But then, Sandra was eighteen years older than me, so she really was from an older generation.

I walked up to the half-glazed uPVC front door and knocked, and the door was opened almost straight away. A woman stood there smiling; she was shorter than me by quite a bit, her hair was very short, she was definitely older but well preserved and nicely made up, well dressed and wearing jewellery. I felt she had made an effort; she looked nice. Quite the contrast to me as I stood there in my jeans and casual top; as usual wearing very little makeup and my hair all over the place. I felt under-dressed, if not decidedly scruffy, and my first thought was, "Maybe we are not alike at all." She was holding a bouquet of flowers in her hand to match those I had brought for her. "Great minds think alike," she said, and held out her arms for a hug.

We hugged for what seemed like a long time. Then she stood back and immediately said, "I meant what I said. I will never do anything to help you find Mother. I've made up my mind." Mixed signals again, and we hadn't even got past the front door. She moved aside and beckoned me into the hallway. There was a doorway straight ahead into the kitchen, and windows looking out towards the back garden. "More flowers", I thought to myself. There was a man in the kitchen getting teacups out of a cupboard. Sandra called out, "Henry, Perry's here." The man in the kitchen turned around. He had a kindly face and an aura of gentleness about him. I decided right away that I liked this man. Later, when Sandra told me they had never argued once in their marriage, I could believe it. This did not look like a man who would argue about anything. "How about a cup of tea? I expect you need one after that drive," he said, kindly.

Sitting in the cosy living room with our cups of tea, I

took the time to look around at my surroundings. I was facing a large wall unit filled with china. I knew the pattern; Royal Albert Old Country Roses. Quintessentially English, and obviously the best china which only came out on those very special occasions. The living room was comfortable, spotlessly clean and nicely furnished; Sandra clearly took pride in her home. Henry told me they had planned to take me out to a local pub for lunch. Sandra added that their daughter Jean would meet us there. I was interested to meet Jean as we were of a similar age. I was also intrigued because she had been quite brusque on the phone. I wondered if we would be at all alike, but I somehow doubted it.

But before lunch we had some talking to do, and Sandra had some reading to do from my adoption file. I handed her the ring binder that now contained the stack of papers. She smiled and shook her head as she read. "Who would have believed this was possible?" She said, still shaking her head. "She did all this, and we had no idea." She read for a few minutes; then she lifted her head, looked at me and said, "She kept this secret all her life. I think perhaps it's best that her secret dies with her." Maybe that's what Sandra thought, but I wasn't so sure it was what I thought.

Later, we went out for lunch. Henry drove us all to the chosen pub in their squeaky clean immaculate little car. He was extremely proud of it and told me so. The pub was one of those chain steak-house affairs, just a short drive of a few minutes from their home. It seemed they were regulars there. I had half expected Jean to be there in the car park to meet us, but she wasn't. By way of explanation, Sandra said, "She was going to try to get away when she could. I expect she'll arrive soon." We went up the steps to the big double doors with the brass handles and Sandra led the way inside.

Lunch was buffet-style, a carvery with three choices of meat and then help yourself to as many vegetables as you wanted. Sandra and Henry insisted I went ahead of them. Henry gave me a nudge whilst I was waiting in the queue and said, "You can have beef, ham AND turkey if you want to; that's what I do." I smiled back at him and decided I would do the same. Sandra said, "Henry likes his vegetables well cooked." And then, turning to him, "I think you'll find the cauliflower is a bit too hard for you, dear." Again, this was so very English; my mum and dad had always preferred their vegetables cooked to within an inch of their lives, but I didn't.

We took our plates piled high with food, as one does at a carvery, back to our table and began to eat. I became aware of someone approaching and looked up to see a woman of about my age walking towards our table. She had very short dark hair, she was slim and very well turned out with carefully applied makeup, and nice jewellery. Jean. Like mother, like daughter I thought. But not like me. Again, I was aware of my slightly underdressed appearance.

"Hello dear," said Henry as his daughter bent to kiss him on the cheek. "This is Jean," said Sandra by way of introduction. I met Jean's gaze. She had icy cold blue eyes. She said nothing. I said, "Jean, I am Perry, your aunt, and I'm very pleased to meet you." I shuffled sideways on the bench seat to make room for her to sit next to me. She gave me a look of cool appraisal and sat down without a word.

Jean immediately started an animated conversation with her mother who was facing her directly across the table; it was something to do with a job interview. She spoke quickly and she didn't look at me once. I felt I was invisible. She said not a single word to me throughout lunch, although I attempted a couple of conciliatory remarks in an effort to get her to speak to me, with no response from her. Even a hello would have been nice, I thought. I couldn't figure out whether she was shy or rude, but I reasoned that it must be awkward for her and decided to give her the benefit of the doubt. She had spoken to me on the phone before, after all. Clipped and brusque maybe, but she had been the first to make contact.

I ate mostly in silence after Jean arrived. The food was good, and I even had dessert. When it was time to leave, we all walked out to the car park together. Jean pecked her father on the cheek and gave her mother a quick hug. "I'll ring you later," she said to Sandra, with a glance at me, the intimation being that she would have something to say about me but not in my presence. This was difficult. Feeling that I had to do something, I put out my hand towards her, to shake her hand. A hug was most definitely out of the question, that much was clear. I said, "I'm so happy to have met you." She stepped back away from me, it was a recoil, and she shot me what I can only describe as a freezing look; I realised this was not going to be an easy relationship to establish. Then she simply said, "Goodbye," turned smartly on her heels and walked away towards her car.

I really didn't know what to make of Jean's reaction, but as soon as we were settled back in Henry's car Sandra said, "She's not a person who demonstrates her feelings. She's a lot like Mother. She doesn't really have any friends." I actually thought Jean had communicated her feelings only too well, but I kept it to myself. We drove back to the house in silence; I don't think any of us knew what to say.

I was seated back in the very English living room with another cup of tea, and Sandra came in with a large, framed black and white photograph. She handed it to me. It was a family portrait of a woman, a man in military uniform, and a small boy. The woman had a round, kind, open face; she was smiling slightly and looking directly into the camera lens. She looked respectable; matronly, even. I thought I knew her from somewhere; she looked so familiar to me, like someone

I had met but couldn't quite place.

Sandra said, "That's her. Our mother," and then I realised stupidly that of course I knew her. I had seen her face before, as a baby. Perhaps from those first nine days after I was born, when we were still in the hospital. I know how fanciful that sounds, but I really felt a connection with that woman whose face as looking out at me from the photograph; I believe the memory must have been etched into my mind and seeing the photograph brought it back to me.

This was my birth mother, Edith. The man in the uniform was Roy, the handsome Master Sergeant she had married, and the boy was my half-brother, George. The portrait had been taken shortly before they left for their new life as a family in America. That must have been how she looked at about the time I was born. I couldn't see any harshness in her face. She looked happy. Not hateful, not hard, not cruel. I asked Sandra if I could have a copy of the photograph. She said she would get one made for me and send it on.

One of my burning questions has always been, how did I come by my name? Edith had named me, and my mum and dad had kept the name because they liked it. It was "me". I asked Sandra if she knew why Edith might have named me Perry. Did she know anyone called Perry who she may have named me after? She said she had no idea.

Distastefully she said, "There were lots of them, lots of Americans. They used to come around to Mother's flat in the evenings, to drink and play darts." She asked me who my father had been. I told her, "His name was Eugene Gallagher." "Ah yes, Gene," she mused. She looked thoughtful. I asked her if she had known him. "No. I just remember because of his name. I always thought it was a funny name for a man. I was only seventeen, just a girl. I didn't like being around them." I thought she might not be telling the whole truth; she had reacted immediately when I had said his name.

Henry said, "I remember him. There were two or three of them that were regulars at her place. They would come around and have a drink." I took out the photograph of the three men from my adoption file and handed it to Sandra, hoping to refresh her memory and maybe find out the names of the other men in the photograph. Perhaps one of them had inspired my name, perhaps one of them was the American with his name redacted in my file who had wanted to marry Edith. "I didn't know anything about that," Sandra said. She looked at the photograph and said dismissively, "No. I don't know who they are. It was a long time ago."

Sandra showed me some more photographs. Her and Henry's son Julian, his wife and their daughter. They were living in Ireland but were planning a move back to England. Julian looked a lot like Henry. There were photographs of Jean's adult children, and more photographs of them as babies and toddlers. Some black and white shots of our mother and brother in America: a tiny well-groomed woman standing next to a tall slim dark-haired man in shorts. The woman was holding a cigarette in her hand. "She always smoked," Sandra said. Then she handed me a colour photograph of an old and proud-looking woman in a wheelchair. "That was Mother, last May, when we visited," she said. I took the photograph and studied it. The woman looked strong and proud, a determined face and there was a hardness to her features that was not evident in the photographs of her as a younger woman. "She hates having her picture taken," said Sandra, as if reading my mind, "You can keep that one if you like."

Sandra told me how Edith's husband Roy had passed away recently. They lived in a senior's complex with various levels of care available. Edith had been in the nursing home and Roy was still living in the apartment they had previously shared, elsewhere in the complex. His death was sudden and unexpected. His car was still parked on the driveway. He had died leaving no Will and all his money was tied up in probate. Edith's expenses were being taken care of by the lawyer who was handling their financial affairs. Roy had money, and it struck me as strange that a military man who had lived an ordered life, saved for his retirement and provided well for his wife and stepson would not have had a Will. Since marrying Roy, Edith had wanted for nothing. Her care was expensive in the nursing home, but they had lived well, and not wanting for anything was the life she had become accustomed to.

More tea and the afternoon passed at Henry and Sandra's. We talked about my life as an adopted child, about my mum and dad, about my life in Canada. I drove home later that day with some photographs and my mind buzzing. I was glad I had gone to meet Sandra, but I felt we hadn't really clicked. I reasoned that was not altogether surprising. We may have been related but we were complete strangers. We didn't know each other at all. I felt the strange reception I had from Jean didn't help at all. I did come away knowing it would be no easy task to find my birth mother. I wasn't even sure I believed she was in Las Vegas. I had hoped that there would be some reassurance for Sandra when we met in person, and that she would understand I wasn't there to cause problems or upset her mother. There was no doubting that Sandra had suffered at the wrong end of her mother's tongue and attitude, probably for most of her life, and I hated the thought that it may have been because she resented her eldest daughter because of the one she had given up. I desperately hoped that I could have the chance to tell Edith that she had done the right thing, and that I had never blamed her for giving me up.

I really didn't know what to make of the encounter with Jean, but the next day I had an apologetic email from her. She didn't want me to think she was being rude. She had just been preoccupied. She said she was excited to think she now had more relatives, as they had always been a very small family. She was looking forward to getting to know me better. This was all quite unexpected, because she had been very distant and cold, and her recoil when I had reached out to touch her could not be put down to preoccupation. I knew in my heart it was not distraction or indifference that had caused her to be so cold towards me; although what it was, I do not know. I still don't. I decided to give her the benefit of the doubt. I replied to her message, saying no apologies were necessary. I would take her at face value and resolve to put our first difficult meeting behind us.

Sadly, there has been very little contact with Jean since then, but I have come to recognise and understand that, for any number of reasons, not everyone will be overjoyed to meet the lost sheep returning to the family fold. This experience with her did definitely prepare me for some more difficult lessons I was to face further along the road.

I talked to Sandra periodically on the phone over the summer months, but she never relented on her decision not to give anything away about our mother. She and Henry were planning to go to America in May to visit Edith, as they did every year. "I am not saying anything to her about this," Sandra had said. "She doesn't need to know."

I asked her for Emma's email address in Nebraska as George had suggested, so that I could send photographs of my family to him. Sandra told me she'd look it up and let me know. She didn't, so I asked again. She said, "I'm sorry. I've spoken to Emma and she's not ready for this. She doesn't want you to have her email address."

I was hugely disappointed, and more than a bit confused by what Sandra had told me. George seemed to think Emma would be pleased to hear about me. I think he may have said she was excited about it. I couldn't understand why she would not be ready to hear from me, either. I was her aunt, not her mother or sister. What could be so bad about that? Unless she was like Jean, I thought. I couldn't shake the feeling that again, maybe this wasn't quite the truth. Either that, or they were closing ranks to keep me away from Edith.

Sandra and Henry flew off to America in May on their annual trip to see Edith and had arranged to meet Emma and her boyfriend out there. They returned four weeks later with more photographs. It was clearly Las Vegas, so that was settled. Edith looked much older than she had the previous year. Her white hair was combed over to one side and she had lost the proud and haughty look. She simply looked very old and frail. Pictures of Sandra and Edith, Emma and Edith, and every combination of everyone who was there with Edith were emailed to me. They cut into my heart. More photographs arrived; Edith in a wheelchair outside a casino with Henry and Emma's boyfriend; Edith in a wheelchair at The Jungle Cafe, flanked by a beaming Sandra and Emma. I don't know if Sandra had considered this but seeing those photographs of them all smiling and holding that old woman's hands really drove it home to me that I was never going to be able to be a part of her life.

Sandra told me that Edith was now suffering from dementia and would never have remembered me anyway. This made me think. If Edith could not remember me, then it would surely not hurt for me to meet her. She wouldn't know who I was, so what harm could it do? I wouldn't announce who I was. I just wanted to see her. I told Sandra that if I went to see her and she did not remember me, then that was fine. If by some strange chance she did remember, and she wanted nothing to do with me, I would accept it. After all, I reasoned, it should have been Edith's decision to make whether she wanted to see me or not; not Sandra's. I put it to her. It didn't work. She still wouldn't tell me exactly where Edith was.

Sandra confessed to having asked Edith about me when she had visited her. She said she felt she had to. This is how she said the conversation went. "Do you know anyone called Perry?" Sandra had asked." "Perry? No. I don't think so," Edith had replied. Sandra said she had told her she had received a letter from someone called Perry who was claiming to be her daughter. "Did you give up a baby for adoption?" She had asked her mother. "Adopt a baby? I didn't adopt a baby," said Edith. "No," said Sandra, "You had a baby. You gave it up." Edith's response was, "Whoever would say such a thing? Me, have a baby out of wedlock? Don't be ridiculous."

Sandra said she had then gone on to test whether her mother really couldn't remember. She had asked Edith about Arthur, who was another son born in between Sandra and George. Arthur had only lived for a few months. It was the first I had heard of this child. Edith had replied, "Arthur? No, I don't know any Arthur."

Apparently, this convinced Sandra that her mother had buried any hurtful memories and had no recollection of them. "She would never have knowingly lied about Arthur," Sandra said. Rather than this bolstering my case for meeting Edith since she wouldn't remember me, this strengthened Sandra's resolve to keep me away. It made no sense to me to keep me away if Edith wouldn't know who I was, because I couldn't possibly dredge up old memories and hurt her. Sandra had said her motivation was to protect Edith, after all. But no. "There's no point in resurrecting all this with her if she can't remember. It's best that her secret dies with her," she said, and not for the first or the last time.

After hearing this, I pleaded with Sandra. I said I would be content to just see Edith with my own eyes. It wouldn't matter that she didn't know who I was, but for me, it would help me to reconcile my past and move on. But Sandra was still adamant that she would never allow this to happen, I could never do this, and she stuck to her resolve that she would never tell me where she was. I later discovered that she had gone much further than this. She had acted to stop me getting access to Edith if I were to succeed in finding her.

Because I'm tenacious I continued to search. Sandra had inadvertently given me some useful clues in conversations along the way. Edith liked to visit Walmart and there was a store within walking distance of the care home. Staff would push her in her wheelchair over to the store, and she would talk to the greeter on the door. She was a familiar face there and Sandra said they all thought she was a sweet old lady. Realising how this contrasted with her own description of Edith's personality, she quickly followed this with, "Little did they know!"

Researching online, I checked for Walmart stores in Las Vegas. There were four, so this narrowed things considerably, although there are literally hundreds, probably thousands of care homes in the Las Vegas area. I searched for homes with the same zip codes as the Walmart stores, then I checked to see which were within easy walking distance. It had to be close by; she was being pushed in her wheelchair and at her age she would have been vulnerable to heat, and it was certainly hot in Las Vegas.

I must confess that sitting in front of the computer one evening after hours of fruitless searching, I stopped hitting the keys and put my head in my hands. It was 2am, and I had been working on this all day. I cursed Sandra out loud for putting me through that. She could have told me in a second where Edith was, but she wouldn't.

I studied the background of that first photograph she had given me of Edith in her wheelchair. The haughty and proud Edith. I thought it must have been outside the care home. I could see the façade of the building in the background of the photograph; it was almost a peach colour with distinctive white lintels over the windows. And venetian blinds in the windows. Square clipped shrubs, gravel beside the pathways. Google Earth is a wonderful tool. You can zoom in at street level and look at buildings. I did this and found a few possible locations, but I couldn't be absolutely sure.

I wrote down the telephone numbers of all the possible care homes. The list grew longer by the day. It was really a hopeless task, but I kept at it. One evening I telephoned every home on my list, but without Edith's last name I didn't get past the receptionists. This was no good. I needed to know her name. I went back to the ancestry website. There are death records for every State in the Union on there. I knew the city Roy had had died in, and I knew the month when he had died. More slips in conversation by Sandra. Oh, she would kick herself for that. There were only three men called Roy who had died that month. I discounted one straight away because he was Hispanic, and I knew that Roy was Caucasian. I looked for marriage records for the two remaining men and came up with nothing. I knew that Roy and Edith had lived in a condominium in the same area as the care home. I searched property records and finally found what I was looking for. A condominium that had been owned by Roy and Edith Thomas and sold a few years previously. There was a care home not two blocks away, and directly across a major road was a large shopping mall with a Walmart store. I knew I had found her. Edith Thomas, there you are.

Having her last name was decidedly useful. I was sure I was right about the care home. I made the call to the home where I believed she was. I asked for Edith Thomas and was politely asked to hold. Then, another person came on the line. I asked again, "Can I speak with Edith Thomas? Is she a resident there?" I was asked to identify myself. I simply said I was a relative calling from England. Then came the response, carefully worded, "No, there is no-one of that name shown in our records as paying for residential care here." Having confirmed the home as Edith's last known address on public records, I was quite certain that she hadn't been moved and she was there but clearly, I was getting nowhere.

After hanging up, I thought about the words used in the response and realised that she wouldn't have been paying for the residential care herself; it was being managed by a lawyer on behalf of Roy's Estate. Clever. I called again and asked to speak to the manager. I insisted that I knew she was there. This time I was told, "She used to be here, but she isn't any longer." I asked for a forwarding address, and was told, "We cannot give you that information without her explicit permission, and since we cannot obtain that, we can tell you nothing further." I suspected then that Sandra had gone beyond her promise of not assisting me in any way. I believed she had told them not to give me any information, and under no circumstances was I to be allowed to speak with Edith.

I tried another avenue. I went looking for Emma on Facebook. I knew she was in Nebraska, and I tracked her down easily now that I had her last name. I sent her a message. I was concerned because Sandra had said Emma wasn't ready to have contact with me, but I thought I'd give it a try. Nothing to lose, she could always say no. But she didn't; she replied straight away confirming that she was George's daughter. She said she was excited to hear from me.

This was most definitely not what Sandra had told me.

Unprompted, Emma sent me her telephone number and I called her. She was bubbly, giggly, outgoing and very friendly. I asked about her visit with Edith earlier in the year. She told me, "I can't tell you anything about grandma. I'm so sorry. Sandra has sworn me to secrecy." Another base had been covered by Sandra, in case I managed to find Emma. How sad. I didn't want to put her in a difficult position, so I told her that I wouldn't ask her any more questions. I was more than a little angry with Sandra. I stopped all contact with her, needing some time to try to understand.

Then, in late summer, I received a phone call from Sandra, out of the blue. She said, "I've been thinking about all this, and I've realised none of it is your fault, or my fault. I want to come and meet with you and talk about this." Perhaps I could be forgiven for thinking she had a change of heart, and my spirits picked up. I thought she had changed her mind and come to her senses. I arranged for Sandra and Henry to stay for a weekend in September at a friend's nearby holiday cottage. I booked a meal out for us all at the local pub, so that we could talk on neutral ground.

I was to be bitterly disappointed. Sandra and Henry arrived at my home in the afternoon, had a cup of tea and met my daughters. I took them over to the holiday cottage to let them settle in, and we went to meet them later for dinner at the pub. Sandra told me that she no longer felt guilty about her decision not to share any information about Mother with me. I hadn't realised that she ever felt any guilt; she had been steadfast from the beginning. Guilt was not something that sprang to mind when dealing with Sandra. She went on to explain that she had realised it was not HER fault; it had been her mother's decision to give me up and to have no contact with me for all these years, and she no longer felt responsible for that. I had no idea that she had felt any guilt or responsibility; she had given no clues of that along the way. I wondered why she had troubled to come all the way here to tell me that. I was feeling hurt and resentful.

I didn't sleep too well that night, struggling to come to terms with Sandra's revelation. I resolved to be brutally honest with her. I had not pushed her or fully spoken my mind for fear of alienating her the previous evening, but the next morning, over breakfast, I told her how I felt. I told her I did not think she had the right to make decisions for our mother. If Mother herself told me she did not want to see me or have any contact with me, then I could and would deal with that. I confronted Sandra about her actions with the care home and Emma. She admitted instructing the care home not to tell me anything. "She's almost blind," she told me, "I didn't want anyone reading out letters to her from a stranger." I tried again to explain my need for some closure; if I could just see her once, I could move on.

I was angry, and I must have sounded more than a little bit desperate, because from across the table, Sandra considered for a few moments what I had said. Then she said, "If you can get to Las Vegas next May or June, when we are there, I will take you to see her. That's all I will do." It wasn't everything I had hoped for from this visit, but nevertheless I jumped at her offer. I would find a way to be there; and at last I would be able to see Edith

Edith passed away that November. Sandra rang me and broke the news three days after she had died. She had already been cremated. There was no funeral, and nothing to mark her passing because, Sandra said, that's what Mother had wanted. "Her ashes have been scattered in the desert," she said. Edith had died alone, in her room, in her sleep. It was a short conversation with Sandra; and it took my breath away. It was a shock. I didn't know what to say. I was struck by the awful reality that Edith had been alive for fully eight months since I had first found Sandra, eight months during which I could have spoken with her, seen her, or even held her hand for a while. I remember saying, "I hope this won't spoil your holiday," as Sandra had told me she and Jean were flying off to Ibiza the next day for some fun in the sun. As it turned out, she didn't go because she got the flu and felt so ill at the airport that she had to come home.

Days later, with the need to get my thoughts out of my head, I sat down and wrote Edith a letter, saying all the things I had always wanted to tell her. It helped me enormously just to get the words out onto paper, but at that time I couldn't face continuing a relationship with Sandra. Perhaps she didn't understand why I withdrew, because she sent me emails saying things like, "If you don't respond within two days, I'll know you've cut me off for good." She asked me if I still wanted the portrait photograph of Edith, Roy and George. I felt she was trying to bribe me, so I didn't respond. She told me that I failed to consider anybody else's feelings, especially hers. I thought that was rich, after what she had done, and I needed time to lick my wounds.

A year on and we were speaking again, and although I still struggled with her motives, I have accepted that she felt she was doing what she had to. She had been ill herself during the year we did not speak, and I was sorry to hear that. I feel that now we have established a relationship on some level, but to forgive is not necessarily to forget. I am trying though, because after all, as Sandra has said to me, it's not every day you find you have a sister you didn't know you had.

6

American Sisters

Louisa was dead; I had ascertained that much from my research. And she hadn't died in prison, either. There were no records of her even being sent to prison, let alone dying there. I was puzzled by this. I wondered if perhaps she had been found criminally insane and had spent the remainder of her life in a secure mental institution. I did some more digging on the internet. I found a Carla Gallagher who had lived at the same address as Louisa. This must have been her eldest daughter, the older blonde girl in the photograph I'd been given by Roseanne. I looked up the address. Google Earth gave me a view of what looked like a very pleasant townhouse on a tree-lined suburban street. Well, that was the mental home theory thrown out of the window. It looked like she had lived her life out anywhere but in an institution. Things were not adding up. If Louisa had murdered Eugene, there would surely have been some punishment. America doesn't treat murderers with kid gloves.

I toyed with the idea of writing to Carla, but it just didn't feel right. I wasn't sure what to do about it, but I did want to find out exactly what had happened on the night that my father had died. I asked Roseanne. She was vague on the details and strangely distant; I felt she was avoiding telling me. She would only say he had been shot five times in the back at point blank range. I put it down to her having been too hurt to bring herself to remember, let alone share it with me. I asked Jolene. She said there was a lot of misunderstanding and confusion about what had happened that night, but again she was short on details. I'm not even sure how much Jolene really knew. She said she remembered getting a phone call that evening. She and her then husband Buck were at a friend's house celebrating New Year's Eve. Her husband had answered the phone. It was her brother Merle. Before anything had even been said, Jolene remembered half-jokingly saying out loud, "What's happened? Did Louisa shoot Rexton?" She was horrified to find out that was exactly what had happened.

I wrote a letter to the local newspaper asking if they had any archived records of either the shooting or the trial. There surely must have been a trial. I had no response. I tried the local Police Department but again I had no response. I didn't seem to be getting anywhere. I knew I would have to find Louisa's daughters to get the answers to my questions. I thought back to Carla and the townhouse, and again considered writing to her. I wasn't sure she still lived there anyway, and I don't know what held me back, but I was drawn to finding who I called American Jean, the other little girl in the photograph.

There were no public records in North Carolina for any Jean Gallagher of the right age. I had guessed her approximate age from the photograph Roseanne had sent me. She was younger than I was, but not by much. There was no birth certificate listed, no marriage details that I could find. If she were not in North Carolina it would be like looking for that proverbial needle in a haystack. She could be anywhere in the United States, or even overseas. She could be dead, too. I imagined all kinds of things; a young girl traumatised by the circumstances of her life, perhaps going off the rails, taking drugs, alcohol, maybe suicide. I didn't know what I might find, or whether she would even want to speak to me.

I thought again about Carrie, the youngest daughter, but I couldn't find her either. I had less to go on with her; I didn't know how old she would be, except that she was younger than Jean. I had no idea what she looked like, except that she was dark haired. It seemed a bit hopeless, so I went back to looking for the elusive Jean Gallagher.

I had recently discovered social networking, and more importantly Facebook. So had Aunt Jolene, and it was a new and easy way to keep in touch. Roseanne and another of my aunts, Martha, got the Facebook bug, too. I used it to find old friends from my previous life in Canada. I found a couple of Jean Gallaghers on Facebook and pulled out the old photograph of the two little girls to compare features and faces. One of the women I had found looked a little like a grown-up version of the young Jean in the photograph and I got my hopes up, but it was just too good to be true and when I contacted her through Facebook Messenger, I quickly found out that it wasn't her.

I tried some of the other social networking sites, and one day I got a hit on a website called MyLife for a Jean Gallagher. She was now Jean Gallagher Brown with a North Carolina address. There were no photographs, just a business address. This potential new name was worth a try on Facebook with its profile photographs. I typed in Jean Brown, set the location to North Carolina, hit the return button and boom, there she was. It was really that simple. A smiling blonde woman of about the same age as me, sitting on the floor of her living room, legs crossed, with a wrapped gift on the floor beside her. From the comments posted on her Facebook Profile, she had just celebrated her 50th birthday. There was no doubt in my mind that this was the little blonde girl in the old photograph with her big sister Carla, now all grown up. She had the same smile. I don't know what I'd been expecting, but she looked quite normal; not crazy, not at all "off the rails". I was happy beyond belief. There she was, my half-sister American Jean. Later I was to find out that her posting a profile on MyLife had been done on a whim and that she rarely used the last name of Gallagher. And she had literally signed up for Facebook only a few days previously.

Before I tried to contact her, I sent an email to Jolene and Roseanne telling them I thought I had found Rexton's daughter Jean. I stopped short of telling them I had found her on Facebook. I knew they could see her profile if I told them how to find her, but I wanted to contact her myself first, and who knew? Maybe she wouldn't even want to talk to me, and maybe she wouldn't welcome them back into her life after more than 30 years. I won't ever forget Roseanne's response to my message telling her I had found Jean. It was headed, U MUST KNOW WITCHCRAFT. I thought this was really odd. What was she trying to say? I was not sure what she meant by it, but she went on to say that she would be very surprised if Jean responded to me after "everything she had been through". Fair enough, I thought, she may be right. But after all that work to find her, I was determined to give it a try. It meant an awful lot to me.

After the "witchcraft" email from Roseanne, I didn't hear from her again for a very long time, and she ignored me when I asked her what was wrong. It obviously had everything to do with me finding Jean, but I decided to put it aside for the time being, trying not to judge or make assumptions, and just give her the space I felt she needed.

It has been a strange experience to read back over those initial exchanges between Jean and me. I was trying to be so careful, so afraid I would put her off with my words;

conscious of trying to say only the right thing, if there is such a thing as the right thing for these circumstances. I was desperately afraid she would ignore me – or worse, tell me to go away and not come back. I had always said I would take whatever came, the good with the bad and I have done that, but I don't know what I would have done if she had not responded. And in fact, I could tell from her actions that she was giving it a lot of thought before she did respond. I had sent her a Friend Request and I could see she had accepted this, and then shortly after, she had "deleted" me, no doubt after she had looked at my profile and seen that some of her aunts were on my Friends List. I knew there had been no contact with them for more than 30 years, and it was becoming clear that perhaps Jean didn't want that to change.

I tried to put myself in her position, which of course I really couldn't because I was short on the facts, but I tried anyway. My first message to her must have come as a shock. She had no idea I even existed, of course. She had no idea of what kind of relationship I had established with her aunts, or what they had told me. I explained that I was Eugene's daughter and had been born in England after he had returned to America. I said I knew of the tragic circumstances in the family, which I hoped she would understand was my way of saying I knew her mother had shot our father. (How do you say that in a less shocking way?) I said that I hoped she would be prepared to have contact with me, and that I had some questions for her.

After she had looked at my profile and then deleted me, I wasn't sure what I should do. I decided I would send her another Friend Request. I wasn't going to give up so easily, although I hadn't thought beyond what would happen if she promptly deleted that one, too. She didn't. She sent me a message back; she said she was sure I knew she had chosen not to have anything to do with her father's family, specifically her aunts and uncles. I didn't know that. I had believed what I had been told; that they had just lost touch because it had been too painful a memory for them all, and they hadn't wanted to conflict the children's feelings. Jean said her father wasn't always nice and that she wasn't sure I would want to know what it had been like to live with him. She sent me her email address. I took this as a positive sign. I replied and said I wanted to know everything – good, bad or otherwise. I explained that I wasn't doing this to make myself feel good and I knew it wasn't a fairytale with a happy ending. I told her everything I knew about Edith and my past, and I left it at that, with the ball squarely in her court.

The biggest surprise came when I got a message from Jean's eldest son Dean. He wanted to know if I looking to build a relationship or just get information. At first I wondered if Jean had asked him to sound me out, but it quickly became apparent that he was acting on his own and that maybe Jean didn't even know that he had contacted me. He told me that his mother had sat him down and told him about me. He was fascinated and said we were like something out of a TV show. I felt an instant bond with Dean, and we emailed back and forth. Jean had told him not to tell Carla or Carrie about me, but he did anyway. That was Dean. He told me not to expect too much from either Carla or Carrie. He said they had all suffered from their upbringing and had dealt with it in different ways. The three sisters didn't really speak to each other much. Carla was reclusive and kept herself to herself, she wouldn't answer the door or the telephone for days on end. Carrie was married, lived in Florida and had dogs which she doted on. They were her life. His mother, he said, suffered from post traumatic stress disorder as a result of what had happened to her. I was beginning to get an inkling of the kind of childhood my sisters might have endured. I didn't say anything to Roseanne or Jolene, but I was thinking Eugene may have been anything but a hero.

Dean told me that his grandmother Louisa was an angel and that they had been very close. She had died of cancer when he was only fourteen. Her marriage to Eugene had always been troubled. He was a violent man, especially when he was drunk. I asked Dean if he knew what had happened when Eugene had been shot. He didn't know, but he went to Carla and asked her what she knew.

Carla was living on her own at the time of the shooting and wasn't a part of what happened that night, but this was her account as she remembered it: Eugene had been out on a drinking binge that night with his younger brother Merle, and Louisa had seen them out riding around in a car. She and her daughters Jean, then nineteen, and Carrie, just thirteen years old, had gone back to the house and there had been a confrontation in the living room when Eugene came home. He had begun beating Jean with his fists. Terrified, Louisa had rushed to the bedroom where there was a loaded handgun kept under the bed. Eugene had followed her and pinned Louisa against the wall. There was a violent struggle and the gun, which Louisa had in her hand, had gone off. Jean had tried to pull Eugene off her mother and had been shot in the hand. When it was over, Eugene was dead, with five bullets in his body. Carrie had been standing in the hallway and had seen everything. Louisa was arrested but was acquitted of murder. The trial hadn't even lasted a day; the Judge had dismissed the case, stating that Louisa had clearly acted in self-defence.

7

The Unexpected Truth

Looking back now, it's amazing how quickly American Jean and I bonded. After Dean and I had been messaging back and forth for a few weeks, she decided to bite the bullet and talk to me. As we started to get to know each other, we discovered how similar we were in so many ways. I felt a connection with her that I hadn't felt with Sandra. Jean and I shared the same biological father, but the similarities didn't end there. There have been many parallels in our lives over the years that are so close it is difficult to dismiss them as coincidence. We have both been married three times, we both have two children. She has sons whereas I have daughters – my eldest daughter mirrors the personality of her eldest son; my youngest daughter reflects the personality of her youngest son. When I later visited her and went into her home, I found we had even chosen the same picture frames. In conversations we finished each other's sentences and we have the same mannerisms. I don't know how those things can be explained.

In December 2009 when I found Jean, she was a captive audience for all my questions because this usually busy, workaholic lady who would normally have had a million reasons not to sit still and think about her past – especially around Christmas – had been slowed to almost a complete standstill by falling down some steps and breaking her foot. The timing of her accident was spectacular, right before I found her. She had nowhere to go and time on her hands and so, in between hallucinatory painkillers, she told me about her life and what it had been like growing up with the father I would never know. What he had been like as a man, who he had become in the later part of his life and how he had died. I knew it must have cost her a lot to look back, relive and share these things with me, and I realised how strong she must be to have forgiven him for he had done, and still love him. She sent me a written account of her life which explained everything. This is what she told me.

"When Mama and Daddy got married, he moved her and Carla to Florida. Mama got pregnant almost right away with me, and I was born there. They separated before I was four years old and Mama, Carla and I moved back to live in a small town in North Carolina. I don't know what he did during the two or three years they were apart.

I have vivid memories of living in a little house by the bus station. I remember going to get the polio sugar cubes and Kennedy being shot, and Daddy jumping the wall from the bus station to the house and seeing me in the backyard playing when he came back to town. He picked me up and took me to the door and when my mom opened the door and saw him holding me, she was scared he was taking me. That's when they got back together and he moved us back to Florida again. My sister Carrie was born the next year.

Daddy worked hard - really hard, and made sure we had a place to live. It might have been lacking in a lot of comfortable things, but it was a house with the utilities we needed. We got a telephone soon after others in the neighborhood did; we got a color TV pretty early on. He did auto-body work most of his adult life, and branched out into real-estate and life insurance. I think he was trying to better himself, although with only an 8th grade education and an Air Force dishonorable discharge, it was probably extremely difficult for him. He went into construction for a good amount of time and when Merle came to live either with or near us, he brought him into it too. He never participated in anything related to us girls that I remember, never attending any school function except my graduation from high school and nursing school (and smashingly drunk at that one). We lived only a couple of miles from the beach, but I don't remember him going with us during the many many many times we went, except when family was visiting. And yet, he took us to Disney World in Orlando the very Fall it opened and took us to places like Parrott Jungle, Monkey Jungle, up into the Smokey Mountains, the Miami Zoo, took me to real life pro-wrestling matches, etc. which really contradicts his parenting style and behavior pattern. It was truly as if he was conflicted and unable to stay on the path he really desperately wanted to be on. As if he wanted to be a family, but never could grasp the concept. And we daughters learned the same...... this was his one success and legacy!

Daddy seemed to have had a real soft-spot for Roseanne and Merle. Merle would come and live with us when he got into trouble and needed to hide out, or had run out of money and luck. Daddy always was there for Merle - trying to help him to do better. And he must have helped Roseanne move up to live close to us for several years also. Mama liked Roseanne. She once told me that Roseanne had a lot of Daddy in her. I'm not sure what she meant; not sure if she meant the "want to do better and be better" or the "to hell with the world I'll do what I want" part of Daddy. I wish I had been mature enough to know I needed to ask more questions about her statement. The problem was, you never knew which Daddy was coming in the door - sober and irritated, or drunk and furious - we learned to kind of determine it by the time of day, or night, and how loud the car door slammed shut. Most of the time, we were securely playing out of sight in our rooms before he got into the house, or pretending to be asleep if it was after bedtime.

Daddy was saved by God's grace in early 1973. We moved back to North Carolina from Florida in March 1971. Mama and us kids had gotten involved in a Baptist church and she was active in the adult Sunday school. I was very active in the youth group - I had been saved a few years prior and really depended on God for daily strength. I was already keenly aware that we couldn't survive this kind of family life without Jesus' help. Daddy had gotten totally out-of-hand with his drinking and was beating on us again. Mama sought help from the church and an older couple stepped in and offered their home for safety if she needed it. The man was a saved alcoholic who had been a lot like Daddy. The point came when Mom needed to get us to safety and we fled again while he was out drinking. When he found out someone from the church was helping her, he was furious and called the pastor to meet him at the church. Daddy had made his intentions to harm him clear, but Pastor Melvin still agreed to meet him. When Daddy walked out of that church office, he was a totally changed man. He was a man free of the demons that had haunted him for so many years, truly sorrowed at the life he had lived and put upon his family. He was a man saved by grace.

The day he was baptized was a day of joy for that entire church body. He joined a lay-witness team and travelled around, telling his story of how Jesus saved him and gave him another chance to be a husband and father. He carried a little New Testament everywhere he went and showed the marked passages to countless people - he didn't want anyone to go through what he'd been through. He and I travelled to Indiana together and we spoke together at a revival about our family life and what God had done for us. The feeling of being a 15 year old and praying with my daddy was just awesome. No words can describe how cool it was. We would laugh and talk about some of the things he'd done when he was drunk, like driving the tow-truck through a neighbor's front yard in the middle of the night and telling the police it was Mama that did it. I talked about how I had hated him and dreamed he'd be dead when he was mean and drunk. We really laughed with him and rejoiced at how that life was over. He had real friends, men who loved him and honored him.

I never noticed at the time, but when I look back I think money and finances slowly became a problem. Daddy changed jobs a couple of times. Mama went to work (another sign to me now that money must have been becoming a problem).... Roseanne had moved up here and

Merle would be around at times.

I graduated from high school and worked part time at a local nursing home, waiting to go to nursing school that August of 1976. Two weeks before I was to leave, I got up early on a Saturday morning to work the first shift. When I opened the fridge to get some milk, there sat a 6-pack of beer. Budweiser. I was stunned - absolutely horrified. I will NEVER *forget that moment. As soon as I got to the nursing home, I called Pastor Melvin. He tried talking to him but for whatever reason, Daddy had made the decision - abruptly and irreversibly - to go back to drinking. We never knew why. Pastor Melvin told Daddy that God had said clearly to him he would take him home; he would end his life before he would allow him to mess up the wonderful things he had used him to do; that Daddy would die before he would bring dishonor to Jesus name. Daddy was dead within 2 years.*

Daddy was a mean and vicious man like we'd never seen after that. I went away to nursing school and he cut off my money. Now I wonder if he was that broke and had no choice and covered it by meanness. I was 16 and without college money and certainly couldn't go back home. I broke down at school during a conference with my advisor - I was scared to death - within a week, the school gave me a full scholarship. I never paid a dime after that. God takes care of us. The nursing home allowed me to work every weekend during my two years of school. That's how I paid for my food, clothing, and gas money. I came home and worked every Saturday and Sunday and then drove back to school. I was at the house as little as possible and out of his path as much as I could be. He seemed to have a special anger towards me - I am not sure if it was because of our closeness in church or because I was breaking away and surviving.

He moved the family four times in the two years I was away at school. I got a job in a nearby town at a hospital that had apartments available. Within two weeks of graduation in June 1978 an apartment became available to me. It was right beside a security guard's apartment. This became important later on. I settled in, never inviting Daddy to my place and only going home to visit when he wasn't there. At some point during this time, Merle was back at the house. I can't remember if he was actually living there or living somewhere else and just working with Daddy, but he was there. I think Roseanne was gone; at least, I don't remember her being around then.

Over Christmas 1978, Mama had gotten the flu. On New Years weekend she was really sick. Daddy and Merle weren't around - it was a holiday and they were off drinking. I went home and stayed with Carrie and Mama on the Saturday night, December 30th. On the Sunday morning Mama had a temperature of over 102, and she was afraid of how Daddy would be when he came home drunk. She was quite pitiful and didn't want to be there to face him. I couldn't leave her there so I left him a nice little note explaining that I'd come home and found her too sick to be by herself with Carrie, and had taken them to my apartment. I left my number and told him we'd be back the next day.

We stopped by my boyfriend's house and got his TV, then went to my apartment. Late in the afternoon, Daddy called. He began threatening us. He said we had thirty minutes to get home or he was going to come and kill us. I called our apartment manager and she called the hospital security guards. They offered to come to the apartment and be present when he got there, but said he had to commit a crime before they could actually intervene. The problem was that we knew we would have to face him sometime; there was no way around it. There was no one that could help. So we drove home. On the way we passed a car that looked like his, but we weren't sure. When we got back to the house he wasn't there, so we just sat and waited. It was after 6pm and getting dark. There was a fire in the fireplace but it had burned down and wasn't very hot, so I'd left my coat on. It wasn't too long before he got to the house and came in. At first he was talking and not too belligerent. I can't remember if Merle came in with him or whether he arrived within a few minutes of Daddy getting there. I don't remember if Merle said he was with him driving to my apartment or not, but that's where Daddy had been. Merle was sitting on the couch across from the fireplace and I was sitting in the chair right next to the fireplace. There was a coffee table between my chair and the couch. Daddy was upset. He said I had interfered by taking Mama to my apartment. As he talked, he got increasingly angry. He went out for a few minutes and when he came back in he was holding a large plastic Christmas door decoration which he said was off my front door; proof, he said, that he had been coming to get me. The decoration wasn't mine; it belonged to the security guard next door. Later, he came to court to testify about it. Daddy threw it into the fireplace to burn but because the fire wasn't very hot it just burned a little, and only around the edges. Because of that it was preserved and became great evidence in court.

All of a sudden, Daddy turned around and knocked me with his fist, knocking me out of the chair and down between the chair and the coffee table. Thank God I had my coat on; it had furry stuff around the neck and cuffs - and as I threw up my arms, he was pelting the fur with all his might, but not striking me in the face because I was protected by the fur. As I went down something hit the coffee table hard, making a loud clunk. It was most likely his fist or knee as he bent down to beat me, but Mama clearly thought she heard and saw my head hit the table and that my scream was from the pain. And she, after almost nineteen years of hell, literally snapped. I remember hearing Merle screaming at him, but I couldn't see anything because he was on top of me, and I was down between the chair and the table. All of a sudden, he was gone running down the hall towards the bedroom screaming that he was going to get Louisa, that she better never run from him like that again. I don't remember seeing Merle or Carrie at that point, only seeing Daddy's back as he ran down the hallway and I ran after him, screaming at him to leave her alone.

The bedroom was at the end of the hallway. There was a chest of drawers, waist high and long, against the bedroom wall, so when you walked into the bedroom it was immediately on your left. The headboard against the back wall was facing towards the doorway. Daddy had a gun that he kept under the head of the bed. We all knew it was there and no one ever messed with it. I couldn't have told you the first thing about it. About the time I reached the bedroom, I heard a shot ring out and suddenly I saw a gun and hands in the air. There was no comprehension as to who was doing the shooting; I just saw a gun and hands. I don't remember jumping for the gun or anything, I just remember seeing my daddy's back and my mama's face; the look of sheer terror on her face. And then hearing more shots, and then absolute quiet; no sound at all. Somehow I was on top of my mama and my daddy, and I could see his hand - it looked to me like he was holding the gun, but in actuality, Mama was holding the gun and he had grabbed her hand. Then sounds; like gurgling, like attempts to talk (or breathe). I bit his hand horribly hard, trying to make him let go of the gun. He didn't move and I bit harder. He still didn't move. Later, those bite marks were evidence that I was trying to make him let go of Mama's hand and the gun, amidst the accusations from his family that he was innocently shot in the back.

Somehow I got up, and Mama got up. Mama was yelling at me to go, to go. I saw Merle and Carrie at the other end of the hallway; Carrie was sobbing. I remember running across the street to the neighbors for help, but they weren't at home. The next thing I remember is being on the front porch but Merle and Mama wouldn't let me go back inside. They said he was going to be ok, but he was dead. And then, the worst look of all on Mama's face when she looked at me and realized I had been shot; during the struggle she had shot me in the hand.

The ambulance arrived and they put me in it and took me away. I was transferred to the hospital where I worked for treatment. Carrie had called my boyfriend and he met me there. He and his family took me back to their house sometime very early in the morning when I was eventually released.

Because I had been injured and taken to hospital I missed what happened at the house later on that night. Merle or Carrie had called the church when I had run across the street. The 7 o'clock Sunday evening service had just begun when the phone started ringing, and the sanctuary was quiet because it was prayer time. Someone stepped out of the service to answer the phone, to be told that Daddy was dead and I was shot and apparently Mama was the shooter. The message was whispered to Pastor Melvin who immediately told the gathered congregation. The entire church began praying as he and two of Daddy's former closest friends hurried to the house. One of them took Carrie to Carla's apartment and told her what had happened. Carrie and Merle both gave statements to the police and then Mama was arrested for murder. Since it was New Years Eve there was no magistrate on duty and Mama had to spend the night in jail. She got out the next day after the church put up bail money.

The gun was a Rossi .38 revolver; a five shot - and he got all five. Once mama started shooting, she didn't stop. That was a good thing; the police found he had a loaded gun in his pocket. He would have surely killed her that night had he not been so quickly incapacitated."

That was Jean's account. Roseanne had completely withdrawn from me after I found Jean and she wasn't responding to any of my messages. Now I thought I understood why. The brother she had worshipped – my father – had ended his life as a violent drunk; killed in a struggle with a woman trying to protect her daughter and herself. Roseanne couldn't – or wouldn't - face the truth. She must have known that Jean would give me a different account of what had happened that night. But why would she say he'd been shot in the back? I now know that the first bullet hit him square in the chest, and that the remaining rounds were discharged whilst he was holding onto Louisa's hand. As he gripped her hand high above her head, with the gun facing downward, the remaining bullets were discharged into his shoulders and upper back, and one went through my sister Jean's hand.

I was shocked by the enormity of it. If I had sat down for hours by myself and tried to think up the most unbelievable set of circumstances I could have imagined, I am not sure I could have topped the truth of it. I wondered how this rift in the family could ever be healed, but I knew it wouldn't be anything I could do or say. I could only hope that I would be accepted by both sides of Eugene's family, and that I could somehow make a positive difference and help to bring them together.

8

Paternal Family

Eight children: five girls and three boys, my father was part of a large family. They were dirt poor; their daddy - my grandfather - worked at the cotton mill and most often drank his paycheque away. There were times when he would come home and beat on the children and their mother. Little wonder that the family I found was damaged and traumatised. I was to discover that each one of the children had found their own way to cope. Some were more successful than others.

Having grown up in a comfortable home in a small village in England, life in the rural South of the United States of America was truly an alien world to me. The people there scratched out a living as best they could; they got by with what they had, which was often very little. The Gallagher children worked in the tobacco fields and the cotton mills to help feed the family. They started young. I would sometimes do summer holiday work in the fruit fields England, but that was for pocket money. What they did was out of necessity. In the small rural towns of the South, life was hard and there were few prospects for a better life. This was how my father had grown up, like his father before him. Eugene Jr. the oldest son of the Gallagher family, had been given his father's name as was the common practice of the day. It dated back to the days of the earliest colonies. Families were typically large and passing the name from father to son was done to ensure that the eldest son would be the one to inherit, should the father of the family die intestate. Eugene Jr. took on more than his father's name. Sadly, he learned the same abusive traits, behaviours and habits from his father before him when it came to raising his own family.

Young Eugene had realised as a teenager that a life working in the cotton mills would not give him a future. He had an 8th Grade education and had left school at the age of fourteen. This was also common, if not the norm, as the more workers there were earning money in the family unit, the better they could make ends meet. Finishing High School would give a young person prospects for a better job and the possibility of a college or university education, but in rural America it was more important to have able-bodied young men working in the fields and the mills. Eugene had worked hard and wanted to better himself as well as provide for the family. He had broken with tradition and joined the Air Force when he was seventeen.

It had always been Eugene Jr. who had looked after his younger brothers and sisters when their daddy came home after getting paid at the cotton mill, full of drink and spoiling for a fight. Eugene had taken them down to the woods and hidden them all away or huddled them under the house with the dogs until their daddy had passed out. He protected them as best he could from their daddy's brutal temper; little wonder that Roseanne would describe him as her hero. She told me she had wanted to die when Eugene left home. He was posted to England with the Air Force in 1957 and he never went back home. He sent money to his mother for the family. After he had returned to America in 1958 with a dishonourable discharge from the military, he married Louisa. She was a Russell who were cousins of the Gallagher family and he had known her before he had left for England.

After they married, he took Louisa and her daughter Carla who was just a little girl, and he moved them down to Florida right away.

Eugene's younger sisters Roseanne, Ruby, Martha and Jolene, were closely bonded. Probably stemming from their difficult and abusive upbringing, they were very protective of each other and were also wary of outsiders. Belle, the oldest daughter, did not seem so close to the other girls. Roseanne and Ruby were close in age, as were Martha and Jolene. The two other brothers, Robert and Merle, split the two sets of sisters. At the time of writing, Ruby, Martha, Jolene and Merle are still alive. Belle and Roseanne have both passed away since I found the family and Robert had died from cancer much earlier, aged fifty.

There is no doubt that the sister relationship within any family is a special one. Studies have shown that growing up with a sister leads to being happier in life, less prone to depression and having a greater ability to handle stress. It's a very special bond under any circumstances. In the Gallagher family the sisters have protected and tried to shelter each other from the abusive circumstances they experienced as children. In adult life the four younger sisters closed ranks behind a defensive shield and developed an "us against the world" mentality. This kind of protective response to abuse certainly serves a purpose but taken to such extremes it has an unhealthy feel to it, stifling the individual personalities within its confines, fostering codependency and making it difficult for the individuals to reach out, to trust, or to experience new things. The four sisters were always watchful for anything that could potentially cause them pain or hurt, and who could blame them?

When I first contacted Jolene, she was very quick to tell me that the sisters had a rule of not discussing or disclosing anything about themselves, not even with each other and especially not with an outsider. In the context of a relationship with me, it would be up to each one to decide whether they would even want contact, and what they each would be prepared to tell me about their own life. That was how it was presented to me, but the reality was if one decided they were against letting me in, it made it almost impossible for any of the others to do so, even if they felt they wanted to. There was to be no sharing of information about each other. So even now there is still much to discover about them as individuals, as not all of them have welcomed contact with me, most notably Ruby.

Belle was the oldest Gallagher child. Although she was still alive when I first found the family, I had no direct contact with her and, as she had married and moved away to Virginia before Jolene was even born, she may have escaped some of the experiences which so profoundly shaped the lives of the younger sisters. It is hard to gauge, as apart from fleeting and vague information about Belle's failing health I know very little of her. I do know that she had a large family of her own and that like Eugene, after she moved away, she stayed away. I am sure she would have had memories of her brother as they grew up together because they were close in age, and I would have welcomed the opportunity to sit and talk with her, but this was not to be. She passed away before I had the chance to meet her.

Merle, the one surviving brother of my father's siblings, now lives in Georgia. Violence and alcohol have shaped and dominated his life. When I found records of him online, the first was a newspaper clipping reporting that he had been sentenced to prison for assaulting a woman. He has spent a considerable amount of time behind bars. Roseanne and Martha always tried to keep tabs on him. He is not always easy to pin down, as he moves around frequently and appears to lead a chaotic life. I know Roseanne bailed him out of debt as well as out of jail on more than one occasion. He was Eugene's sidekick and his drinking partner. The men in the family all seemed to have had a problem with alcohol. Merle was there the night that Eugene died. He witnessed what happened and gave a statement to the police. Later he made threats towards Jean, and she has never forgotten it. She is still afraid of him. In the photographs I have seen of him as a young man, he had an angry look about him. He was intense and stood with a clenched jaw and clenched fists. A more recent photograph I have seen of Merle shows an old man; thin and tired-looking, hard to equate with that violent young man in the older images. To the best of my knowledge, Merle has never spoken of that terrible night, which I believe in many ways has fed the mistrust and misunderstanding that exists within the family to this day.

Roseanne was the next oldest daughter. She lived in Virginia not too far from Belle, but many miles away from Martha and Jolene. Roseanne also had a troubled life, several marriages and two husbands that left her widowed. She also had an alcohol problem when she was younger but found a personal faith in God in later years which seemed to profoundly change her. She was the closest to my father of all the children and never really recovered from losing him. For years she struggled with feelings of anger and bitterness towards her best friend Louisa, who she described as being like a sister to her. Roseanne then felt doubly betrayed when Eugene died; she lost her brother, but she was also faced with the fact that it was not a stranger who had taken his life; it was someone she cared deeply about. This must have been deeply conflicting for her, and Roseanne withdrew completely from Louisa and her children rather than deal with it.

The unexpected contact from me, a total stranger, yet a daughter of the brother she had loved so much, forced

Roseanne to confront a lot of feelings which she had buried very deeply. Some, I believe, were too painful to be faced. Initially she was surprisingly open with me, pouring out her feelings in lengthy messages which were so full of pain that they cut me to the core. She told me she had never written anything down like that about her life before. It must have been extremely hard for her and to say that her pain simply radiated from the words I was reading is the closest I can come to describing it. She stopped writing to me very suddenly, and I believe it got too difficult to confront her painful memories. Either that, or she was reminded by Ruby that I was a stranger, and she was giving too much of herself away. She never explained and I was hurt by her withdrawal, because not only did I start to feel like she was a friend, she also seemed like the best placed person to tell me about my father. Her memories when she explained them, made him real to me. After a lengthy period of silence, Roseanne did re-establish contact with me but on a different level and from that point on it was an arms-length relationship. The closeness and spontaneity of her messages were lost and whenever I asked anything which she felt challenged her, she ignored my questions completely.

Ruby is the self-appointed keeper of Mama's Family Photograph Album. The other sisters seem to have been heavily influenced by Ruby and perhaps even a little afraid of her. Certainly, they were careful not to do or say anything to upset her. I know very little about her. She seems to be an extremely private person and apart from the one indirect contact refuting my request for the two photographs in Mama's album, she has never responded directly to me and the other sisters have shared little about her. I had really hoped Ruby would be prepared to allow me to see the photographs of "the little girl in England" with Eugene and the child's mother. I believe Ruby also has a framed photograph of Eugene which always hung in his office, and again I would love to see that. I don't pretend to understand why she would completely shut me out, but I have no choice but to respect her feelings. I am learning to accept there is nothing I can do or say to make her change her mind. I can't change the way things are.

As a child, my sister Jean had been very fond of her Aunt Ruby. She called her, "My favourite Aunt". Jean said she regretted losing touch with Ruby and had often wondered what had become of her. After American Jean and I had got in touch, she asked me what I knew of Ruby. I was unable to tell her much. I told her about the photographs in Mama's photograph album and explained how important it was for me to be able to see them. Then, when I was planning to visit North Carolina in 2010, Jean decided to write a letter to Ruby. I think she thought it would be fitting for the two of us to go together and visit her. She was the one person on that side of the family that Jean would be prepared to meet in person. She did not want to meet any of her other aunts as she clearly did not trust them. In her letter to Ruby, Jean poured out her heart about her feelings for her and told her what she felt she needed to say. She asked if we would be able to visit her together when I was over in America. There was no reply from Ruby for a few weeks, then Jean received a notification of a registered letter. She went to pick it up at the post office. It was from Ruby. She opened it. When she saw that the letter began "Dear Mrs. Brown", it was clear right away that we would not be welcome. I am sure this must have wounded Jean deeply, but she later told me that Ruby's letter had at least been honest, and she had written it in a classy way. I think Jean is a very gracious lady to accept being rebuffed after being brave enough to reveal her heart to her favourite aunt.

Months later I followed Jean's example and wrote Ruby

a lengthy letter of my own, trying to explain my feelings and asking her to reconsider her decision to not allow me to see her parent's photographs. I also suggested that she could just lend the photographs briefly to one of her sisters so that they could be scanned and emailed to me. She never replied, but ever the optimist, I am still holding onto the hope that the situation with Ruby may change in the future, but for now that door seems to be firmly closed.

I had been in regular contact with Jolene since the day I found her photograph on the internet. I felt a closeness to her before I even really knew her. I felt we were as close as two people could be without meeting each other and that there was a bond between us. She was always forthright and told me if she didn't want to answer a question. I appreciated her candour and honesty. During the time I had struggled with my feelings towards Sandra, and again after Edith had passed away, Jolene had given me a lot of support. She may not have known it, but she had just the right words for the situation. She told me, "We have to accept that there are not always happy endings, sometimes there are just endings". It was so perceptive and true. I valued the relationship I had with her. I often think it was a kind of miracle that led me to her first – the outspoken, honest and caring woman who finds it difficult to trust but wears her heart on her sleeve. Had it been one of the other aunts, I am not sure there would have been an open door to my birth family at all.

From the moment I first saw her face on my computer screen I knew Jolene was a special lady. She was the first person I had ever looked at who bore a physical resemblance to me and that alone made her special in my eyes. She had only been a small child when my father had left the family for England, and her memories of him were those seen through the eyes of a little girl. He was so much older than she was. Nonetheless, she had made him real to me, talking of things he had done; jokes he had played on her, games he had played with her and how he had got mad with her one day and chased her through the pecan orchard.

Jolene, like the others, has had more than her fair share of problems, from abusive relationships to learning to live with bipolar disorder. She told me she believed her father and brothers were also bipolar and had used alcohol to self-medicate. It makes sense to me. Jolene does not drink, but she has had problems with anger in the past. She has a core of strength and is a beautiful lady inside and out with a big heart, a true example of a courageous person overcoming huge hardships by the sheer strength of will and character, and as she would say, by God's Grace.

I didn't know what to make of Martha. She wasn't very communicative with me at first, but I felt there was something there. We exchanged emails but it wasn't on a regular basis and it wasn't really on a personal level. I felt there was something holding her back. I was happy to take what I got though. It certainly wasn't a negative experience. Roseanne, although guarded about her sister Martha, had told me that she was married to a good and caring man, and that she had grown-up children. But to me she seemed like a closed book. I knew very little about her, and she never once mentioned Eugene to me, which I found slightly odd.

I had arranged to fly out to North Carolina to meet Jean, and as I thought at the time, my aunts Jolene and Martha. I did not anticipate that I was to feel the full brunt of the effects of the protective sisterhood about a week before I was due to leave. I had excitedly planned my trip for some time. I was looking forward to meeting some of my biological family, seeing where they had grown up and hearing first-hand their stories and memories. I had arranged to stay with Jolene for a short time and visit with Martha who lived nearby. I knew I wouldn't be seeing Ruby, who also lived in the same town as Martha and Jolene, or Roseanne, who had already made her excuses although she knew I was coming. I was sad about that and recalled how she had once said she would love to sit with me and just "talk and talk". I felt it was a missed opportunity because she, out of all of them, was the closest to Eugene and had so much she could have shared with me. But I was excited to meet at least some of the family and so I was devastated when out of the blue, a week before I was due to fly out, Jolene sent me an uncharacteristically blunt email saying that she would be busy and would not be able to see me when I was there.

Of course, I knew immediately that something was wrong. At first I wondered if she was ill, and straight away I contacted Martha by email. Martha's response came back very quickly, and she couldn't have made it any clearer. Jolene was fine, she wasn't ill. Wasn't it clear enough that she just didn't want to see me? And by the way, she, Martha didn't want to see me either, or hear from me again. It was a gut blow. I didn't know what to do. I was going to be flying half-way around the world and suddenly I wasn't wanted there. It took my breath away. This was the sisterhood closing ranks and taking charge, and it was at that moment that I recognised it for what it truly was. Aside from Edith's passing, this was the greatest disappointment of my journey so far.

I contacted Jean. She thought it was because of her. She said that maybe if I stopped contact with her, they would reconsider. I said, no way. I was still coming to see her, and nothing was going to change that.

I was devastated, but the tears were done I decided to send Jolene a message. I knew in my heart that she wouldn't have been behind this and I thought I knew her well enough to expect some honesty if I confronted her. I wrote her a message. I told her I knew this wasn't because she was busy;

I knew what this was about and I was so very sorry it had happened, and that I still cared about her. I told her I was trying to come to terms with it, and that I had just wanted to see her in person. I didn't want to cause her or her sisters any pain. I was determined to carry on with my trip, I was coming to meet Jean and visit some of the places that Eugene had known, and if necessary, I would do it on my own, but I was coming anyway.

There was no immediate response from Jolene. My heart was really in my boots, and I thought I had lost her. But I could not know or understand the forces at work; or more surprisingly what was happening with her sister Martha, whose harsh words had really hurt me. It turned out that after Ruby had received Jean's letter, there had been a meeting of the four aunts; Ruby, Roseanne, Martha and Jolene; and together they had decided to close ranks and shut me out. It was a step too far to come face to face with me, and the memories that came with me. They were not ready for it, so shutting me out was what they decided to do.

Interestingly, over the next few days, Jolene and Martha were each brought to the realisation that they had made the wrong choice. Independently of each other, they agonised over what to do. Then, at precisely the same moment they had emailed each other – both saying they thought they had made the wrong decision. Their emails crossed in cyberspace. They phoned each other; they had both changed their minds and wanted to meet with me but were worried I would not forgive them. For perhaps the first time in their lives, a brick or two had been knocked out of the protective sisterhood wall.

Jolene, needlessly afraid of what my reaction might be, emailed my oldest daughter and asked her if she thought I would still be prepared to meet up. My daughter called me. I didn't think twice about it; I told Jolene I was still coming;

we would meet and we would work things out.

9

America Bound

I had planned my visit for June. I had already set aside the time from work, because that was when I had previously planned to fly to Las Vegas to meet Sandra and see Edith. That had all changed when Edith passed away the previous November. So I was all geared up for a June trip. Flights were reasonably priced from London and after some online bargain-hunting I booked a direct flight to Raleigh-Durham in North Carolina. On the map it looked strategically placed, about equidistant from my half-sister Jean and my aunts Jolene and Marth. It was arranged that Jean would meet me at the airport and I would go to stay with her initially. I was excited, but I was also apprehensive after the events of the previous week. In the back of my mind, I wondered whether I would be left waiting at the airport with no-one there to meet me and nowhere to go or stay. At worst, I reasoned, it would be a chance to see North Carolina and have a bit of a holiday.

The morning of my departure arrived. As usual I was travelling on a shoestring budget, so I had booked a seat on the early morning National Express bus from Exeter, direct to the terminal at Heathrow Airport. The bus was the cheapest way to get around. The timing was meticulous; I could hop off the bus, drop off my bag, hop on the plane and be off on my American adventure – all within the space of an hour. I was already checked in for my flight and had confirmed my seat assignment, all done the previous evening online to facilitate smooth sailing on my day of travel.

The bus was due to depart at 4.35am. I had left home before 3am for Exeter and I arrived with my bag in good time. Other passengers for the bus were hanging around at the bus station. Two young Asian men, sitting in the waiting room chattering away excitedly in a language I didn't recognise. A middle-aged couple sat in the Waiting Room opposite me; she was travelling, he wasn't. They were squabbling about her bags. The Heathrow bus pulled into the terminal right on time. There was a scramble to get the luggage into the compartment underneath the bus, a bit of a free-for-all with the bus driver standing idly by while we jockeyed for position to get our bags on as soon as possible. Those with their bags on first could step straight up to the bus door and be well placed to get a good seat on the bus for the long drive to London. I emerged from the luggage melee third in line, behind the woman who had been bickering with her husband. The driver checked our tickets as we boarded and then we were on the bus. It was already quite full, having started in Plymouth and then collected more passengers at previous stops on the route to Exeter.

I settled into a window seat about midway along the bus and looked at my watch. Good timing. Five minutes left before we were due to depart. A large older man plonked himself down onto the seat next to me with a loud sigh. He nodded at me and grunted a greeting. I politely smiled and turned my attention back to the window. It was still dark outside, although I could see the beginnings of the sunrise on the eastern horizon. Minutes were ticking by and I became aware that it was well past the time that the bus should have left. At the front of the bus, the driver was arguing with a young man who had a ticket but nowhere to sit on the bus. The seats were all taken. The bus was either overbooked or there was a mistake with someone's ticket. The driver began walking up the aisle asking to inspect our tickets again. This wasn't good news – I hadn't allowed for too many delays in my timing so I hoped this would be quickly resolved. The driver checked the large man's ticket, and then mine. We were all in order. He checked everyone's tickets and they appeared to be all in order too, so looking slightly baffled, he walked back to the front of the bus and resumed his argument with the young man. Then he made a call on his mobile phone, speaking loudly and obviously agitated. He put his phone down, walked back up the bus aisle and began checking our tickets all over again. You have to have lived in England to understand how this sort of situation can happen. We Brits love a good disagreement, especially if it makes everything run late. But for me on this day, things were not looking good. The sun was coming up fast now and we were already twenty minutes late. My flight connection was tight, and I didn't want to miss the plane.

The driver was now gesticulating and arguing with a man four rows back from the front of the bus. The man was travelling with a woman and a small female child, and there seemed to be a language problem. I could hear the driver telling the man that they needed to get off the bus. "You are on the wrong bus. WRONG BUS! You leave, PLEASE!" The man and his family did not speak English, and it seemed they didn't understand it very well either, because they weren't moving. There was a lot of shouting and waving of arms and protesting but eventually the man stood up, grabbed his child by the arm and hauled her down the aisle of the bus towards the door. The woman was dragging a bag along the aisle behind them. They finally got off the bus and the doors closed behind them with a hiss of air. The young man took his seat. The bus was silent. I think everyone breathed a sigh of relief. The driver, back at the front, settled into his seat, started the engine and we were backing out of the bus bay, finally on our way.

We had a brief stop for coffee at a motorway service area, which thankfully interrupted the snoring of the large man beside me. I was glad of the break but keeping a close eye on my watch. I should be alright for time so long as there were no major traffic jams ahead of us. With luck I should just make the cut-off time for the baggage drop. Back on the road at 7.10am, a cup of coffee in my hand and the man in the seat beside me already snoring again. All was clearly well in his world. The sun was fully up now, and I was finally on my way to North Carolina.

There was another fight for the luggage after getting off the bus at the airport, and then I was off through the endless corridors of Heathrow, dragging my bag on its tiny built-in wheels towards the Drop-off Zone, Security and my assigned Departure Gate. My bag was weighed and dropped off, my hand luggage examined, my shoes taken off and everything in my pockets put into the plastic tray and onto the conveyor belt at the security checkpoint. Little clear plastic zip-lock bags containing toothbrushes, toothpaste, strange-coloured liquids in small see-through bottles were lined up in the plastic trays waiting to be examined and go through the x-ray machine. A few steps forward through the metal-detector gateway – thankfully no beeps for me this time, shoes put back on, pocket contents replaced, a nod from the very serious looking security man, and I was on my way to the Departure Lounge with just a few minutes to spare.

I parked myself on a hard, plastic seat next to a very large gentleman in a green camouflaged military uniform. He had very, very shiny boots. When I say he was large, I mean he was built like an American style refrigerator, one of those massive ones with the side-by-side doors for fridge and freezer. He was huge and muscled, not at all fat, just a very large man. He smiled at me. It was a big smile, like everything else about him. Big. I felt small, tiny in fact. He started talking to me; he called me "Ma'am". I loved his Southern accent. He was telling me that he was going home for his youngest child's "Grad", "Last one out the door," he said, in his velvety voice. I wondered if that's what everyone sounded like in North Carolina. I hoped so. He was going to Fayetteville, where Jolene lived. There's a big military base there; Fort Bragg, one of the biggest military installations in the world. I told him I was going to meet my biological family in North Carolina and that we had never met before. He smiled. "Y'all have a great time," he said, as we were called up to board the plane.

We took off on time. I was in row 28, another window seat. There were two older American gents in the row in front of me. They kept me entertained on the flight, bickering with each other and flirting shamelessly with the pretty flight attendant. They reminded me of Walter Matthau and Jack Lemon in Grumpy Old Men. The grumpy one of the pair, whose name was Larry, looked as if he was still wearing his pyjama top. "You two know each other, right? You are friends?" said the flight attendant, tongue-in-cheek. They started telling her how they had met in Puerto Rico in 1946 and been inseparable ever since. They were quite the comedy duo. I wondered where home was for them.

TOUCHDOWN as they say in America, and we landed perfectly on time, right to the minute. It had been a long flight, but I had arrived. Stepping off the plane and following the signs for Arrivals, I wondered what lay ahead of me on this trip. I headed into the Women's Washroom to quickly freshen up.

Almost twenty minutes later I was standing at almost

the back of a very long line-up of arriving passengers, not having moved very much at all. This was the busy Arrivals Hall and we, having disembarked from various international flights, were shuffling back and forth, back and forth, along lines of rope barriers which eventually opened out at a row of booths at which sat unsmiling Border Agents who were processing us in turn. We all had to be fingerprinted, photographed and interviewed about our business in America. United States passport holders had been filtered away to the right-hand side of the Hall and were being processed far more quickly than we unfortunate international arrivals, at lightning speed in comparison. I had seen the large back of the uniformed refrigerator-sized military man with whom I had spoken earlier disappearing through the double doors, where no doubt his family were waiting to meet him. I don't know I came to be so far back in the line-up, because I was off the plane quickly enough, but after what I had thought was a quick stop at the Ladies it seemed like there were now at least two hundred people in front of me. I had by then been travelling non-stop for thirteen hours from my home in North Devon, on the bus to Heathrow Airport and then the plane to Raleigh-Durham. I was tired and I just wanted to get through those double doors on the far side of the booths.

Waiting out there beyond those doors was a woman I didn't even know existed until eight months before. I had never actually spoken to her, but we had been sending each other photographs, messages and emails since I had found her on Facebook. She is another daughter of the father I never knew; ten months younger, and blonde whereas I am dark. Would we even like each other? What if we don't hit it off? What if she's not even there? Perhaps she won't even show up. And then what? My mind was racing and my anxiety level was getting well into the red zone.

There was a young woman close behind me in the shuffling queue. I didn't remember seeing her on the plane, which surprised me as she was very striking in appearance; tall – over 6 feet – exotic-looking, olive-skinned, dark hair and eyes. She was wearing a very short startlingly bright red dress. I glanced down at her feet, just behind mine, which like everything else about her seemed larger than life. Her toenails were painted red, like her dress, and her large feet were barely encased in black Romanesque sandals. She had been in the Women's Washroom at the same time as me. She must have been really squished into the standard sized cubicle where she had been getting changed into that dress. She had fairly popped out of the cubicle when the door opened as I was washing my hands, and she stood there for a moment in front of the mirror fussing with her hair, moving strands of it this way and that. She must have been carrying that dress and those shoes in the plastic grocery bag that she is now firmly gripping. Strange, I had thought. All that effort with her appearance and I would have expected a Michael Kors handbag, or a Dolce and Gabbana tote, rather than a Tesco grocery bag with its blue stripes. Probably there were sweatpants and a hoodie in that bag. She had obviously travelled incognito and had transformed herself into a bright and beautiful vision that you could not possibly miss. And here she was standing inches behind my drab, tired, weary self. She was fidgeting. She looked nervous, pensive, and I wondered what her story was. She obviously wanted to make an impression on whomever she was meeting on the other side of those doors. She checked her makeup in the mirror of a small powder compact, snapped it shut and for the tenth time nervously smoothed down her dress over her long thighs with her long fingers. She also had really long legs.

Shuffle, shuffle some more, and then finally I was beckoned forward to the booth directly ahead of me by the

Border Agent sitting there. There were several extra booths in operation by then, as it was becoming apparent that we would be there for a very long time if they didn't start to move things along. I felt like I'd been there standing for an hour at least, musing about the tall girl and some of the other passengers in the line, to pass the time. I'd also been watching the uniformed officers process people through, one at a time. Those Border Agents were not at all welcoming. They were all business and they didn't smile. The tall girl had somehow got in front of me and was towering over the seated Border Agent at the booth to my left. "Good," I thought to myself, having already decided that the officer at that booth looked particularly hostile. I could hear him talking as he looked up at her asking the same questions that he'd been asking everyone. All business. "Have you ever been to the United States before? What is the purpose of your visit? How long will you be staying? Stand over here, ma'am, in front of the camera." Flash. "Good. Now put your hand on this screen. Good." I looked at the officer who had beckoned me forward. He was actually smiling at me. Being bold, as I stood on the spot for my photo to be taken, flash, and put my hand on the fingerprint scanner, I told him, "I'm coming to see my sister. We've never met each other before." I looked over to the double doors again and saw a family with small children going through. The door closed quickly, and I couldn't see what was on the other side. The officer looked up from my EU passport. He said, "Is that so? She's out there now?" I said, "Yes. She's waiting just the other side of those doors." He smiled again. "Well, that's somethin'," he said, "Y'all go out there and meet her." He handed me my passport back, still smiling. I thanked him and walked through the doors.

10

Grits and Okra

Time to take stock and reflect. I'm borrowing my nephew Dean's bedroom at my sister Jean's house. It has been an awfully long time since I left my home in Devon and I've gone more than a day with no sleep. I'm not sure exactly what my biological clock will make of this. The king-sized bed is made up and ready for me, with extra throw cushions, but although I am exhausted, I'm not ready to sleep yet. I am buzzing. It seems like I've already been here for ever; so much has happened in the short while since I walked through the doors at the airport that my perception of time itself seems to have been altered. My head is spinning with the emotion of it all. I need some time to think it all through before I can allow myself to sleep.

I had walked through those doors at the airport not knowing what I would find on the other side. My experience with Sandra back in England had made me apprehensive and cautious. I wasn't sure whether I dared to hope for more with my American sister. I pushed ahead through the doors with my bag banging along behind me. My eyes were straight away drawn to a dazzlingly bright blue Hawaiian-style shirt being worn by a man with dark hair, lots of dark hair, and a moustache, and matching bright blue eyes. He was waving as walked towards me, smiling. Suddenly I was laughing and crying at the same time. It was Rob, my sister's husband, I recognised him straight away from photos I had seen of him on Facebook. Behind him, looking like she was trying to hide, was a blonde woman with shoulder length blonde hair. Then she was getting to her feet and in seconds she was there, and we were hugging and crying. My sister, Jean. We stepped back and looked at each other. She was shorter than me, slimmer, but there was no mistaking the resemblance. We laughed, knowing we had been thinking the same thing. Rob took my bag and Jean and I walked out of the airport together, holding hands, to their people-carrier in the parking lot, chattering excitedly to each other like we were two old friends who hadn't seen each for a while. It was such a contrast to my first meeting with Sandra.

Not thinking, I walked to the wrong side of the van. "Are you driving, sis?" More laughter. Of course, silly me – the steering wheel is on the other side of the vehicle. I'd been away from North America for too long, I thought. My bag was thrown in the back, I was seated in the front, Rob was driving and Jean was sitting behind me, talking and laughing. No, this wasn't like meeting Sandra at all. I was so relieved, and more than a little bit happy. Jean said was hungry, "Rob, Rob – I need to eat. Let's find somewhere to eat." She asked me, "What do you feel like eating?" I looked at the bedazzling array of restaurants along the highway. Burgers, steak houses, fried chicken, ribs, barbecue, Krispy Kreme Donuts…it was all a little overwhelming for me, used to rural Devon where it was a ten mile drive to the nearest McDonalds.

We pulled into the parking lot of "The Blue Diner". It looked good to me. There was a huge red flashing neon sign advertising the restaurant at the roadside, beckoning us to come inside with promises of $5.99 "Specials". Blinking red neon eyes complete with eyelashes creeping up from the bottom of the sign to the middle, blinking, then flashing, then disappearing. And starting all over again! Rob parked the van and we went inside the restaurant.

The menu may as well have been in a foreign language. Pulled Pork Sammy. What was this? In for a penny, I thought, and ordered it. Jean ordered the spaghetti, Rob ordered okra. What on earth was okra? My "Sammy" arrived. It was the most wonderful tender slow cooked barbecued pork, in a bun. To call it pork in a bread roll wouldn't have done it justice, so what else could it be but a Pulled Pork Sammy? It came with a side of "slaw" – not the insipid and somewhat acidic concoction of cabbage and carrots that we call coleslaw and are used to having in Britain, or even Canada; this was a tangy spicy crispy wonderful cabbage and cider vinegar dish. I learned that this was the "western" North Carolina version of slaw, differing from the eastern variety – the cabbage is cut differently, the ingredients slightly different, with spicing and colour variations. They take their slaw seriously in North Carolina and there are strong feelings among the people of this State about which slaw the best. In Britain, this would be comparable to the Devon or Cornish pasty arguments, or the dreaded Battle of the Clotted Creams. It matters if you are from Devon or from Cornwall. This visit was going to be a food experience if nothing else, I thought, as I tucked into my pulled pork. "Have you had okra before?" asked Rob. Small green elongated lightly battered things in a pile on a plate. It didn't look very appetising and it could have been anything, and no I had never tried it. Apparently, it was a vegetable. Jean and Rob stared at me so intently as I selected a small piece to try, that I thought they were setting me up for some kind of trick – but no, it was surprisingly good. We laughed again.

When we left the Diner, Rob tried to capture a photograph of the flashing eyes on the sign but couldn't get them – every time the sequence changed, he kept missing the eyes as they flashed. We laughed some more, got into the van and drove to their home in Greensboro.

Their house was on a cool tree-lined street, a mailbox at the end of each driveway, the red, white and blue of the Stars and Stripes gently fluttering in the breeze from flagpoles on the very green front lawns. It had recently been Memorial Day and the flags were still proudly flying. Nowhere on earth are there people more patriotic than Americans. As we turned into their driveway I saw there was a large sign taped to the double garage doors. "WELCOME, BIG SISTER PERRY" in huge multicoloured lettering, and signed by all the family. What a wonderful greeting. Jean explained they had made the sign to take to the airport but had forgotten it in the excitement to get there. She had called home to get one of her boys to put it up on the garage door. We laughed and took photographs by the sign, before going into the air-conditioned cool of the house. More surprises inside, a packet of English ginger-nut biscuits on the kitchen counter to make me feel at home, to have with my cup of English tea which they had bought. They had gone out of their way to make me feel at home. After my long journey, I wanted to cry at their kindness.

After more excited chatting and laughter – after all, we had a lifetime to make up for – Jean and I went for a walk around the neighbourhood, drinking red wine out of plastic cups. The cool of the evening air was refreshing; it was remarkably quiet for a suburban street, so different from the noisy cities and towns on Britain that I was used to. We could have been out in the countryside; there was a pond with a heron looking for fish, and turtles perched on the rocks catching the evening sun. It was wonderful, and just what I needed after such a long and stressful day.

And so I wrote all this down in my journal before

climbing into bed. With the ceiling fan silently turning above me, I was laying there on my back in that king-sized bed that seemed a mile off the floor and the gentle breeze was blowing over me as I reflected on the day. My mind was still buzzing, and I was sure I wouldn't be able to sleep. Jean would be going to work in the morning, but I had a lunch date with Dean, and Rob would be home after lunch. I was looking forward to meeting my nephew, the one who had so openly reached out to me after my tentative first contact with his mother.

I awoke at 4.30am. I was wide awake, realising it would be 9.30am back in England with the time difference. Still on English time, then. I lay there watching the spinning ceiling fan for a while, before dropping off to sleep again. I woke up again at 8am, feeling much more civilised and ready for the day ahead. I showered, marvelling at the water pressure after the sometimes barely-dribbling shower experiences back in my old Devon cottage with its ancient plumbing. The house was quiet and peaceful. I went downstairs to the kitchen and poured a cup of coffee. My cup had been carefully placed beside the coffee maker. So thoughtful. Jean had left me a note on the kitchen counter, complete with cell phone numbers in case I needed anything. I was touched.

I walked through my sister's house with my cup of coffee in my hand, getting a feel for who she was. There was a framed photograph on the wall in the living room of a beautiful middle-aged woman, smiling. The glass was damaged, with a small perfectly round hole in it. I realised this must be Louisa. She was dark haired, almost olive-skinned and this surprised me. I don't know why I had thought she would have been blonde; perhaps because of the photograph of the two little girls, Jean and Carla, both so fair. I could see Jean in her mother's features. There was a framed photograph of a flower on a shelf in the dining room which almost exactly matched one that I had at home in my own dining room. The frame was identical, the photograph just a little different. I was struck by the strangeness of this; we lived so far apart, we had different lives, different upbringings, never knowing the other and yet here, by strange coincidence was a small item which we had both chosen which was almost identical and placed in the same rooms in our respective homes, thousands of miles apart.

Dean breezed in at 11am. So tall, well over 6 feet, handsome, Southern. I loved his accent. We went off in his low slung black sporty car for lunch at a pizza restaurant. He laughed at me when I took a photograph of the pizza, laughed at my accent, laughed at my English sayings. In between slices of pepperoni pizza, he kept making me say things over, and over again, laughing. He told me about school, his girlfriend, his brothers, his ambitions. After we had eaten, he drove me back to the house and we sat on the deck in the sun, talking some more. We had a great time, but it was all too short, he had to get back to school for afternoon classes. We made plans for an evening out with some of his friends at an Irish pub. I wondered what a North Carolina Irish pub would look like.

Later, Rob and I went for a drive to the Farmers Market on the edge of town. I don't know what I had expected, but I had never seen anything quite like this before. It was a huge place, acres of covered market stalls and acres of parking lot. It was quiet today, Rob explained, being a weekday. You couldn't get near the place on a weekend. It was a fruit and vegetable assault on the senses. Peaches, piles of them. We tried one – they let you do that, select a peach and the vendor will cut it for you with his sharp little knife, and hand you a piece of sweet, juicy heaven. Grown in the sandhills of North Carolina, I had never tasted a peach so sweet before. I bought some. Tomatoes – huge gnarly things, all bent around. Little tiny round ones, strange dark red ones, orange acid-free ones. Tomato overload. I went to see a wizened old tomato seller; he had very few teeth and looked like he'd grown up in the field with his produce. He was leaning on a cane beside his table which was piled high with the biggest, most irregular shaped tomatoes I had ever seen. I told him I was visiting from England. He pointed at his tomatoes with his cane. "They's German-Johnsons," he said, "You know how they get to look like that?" Captivated, I said I had no idea. "They gets a good beating with the uuuugggly stick," he said, "Yep, I beats 'em reeal good", showing me a wide toothless grin. "Me, I only eats them little round 'uns", leaving me to wonder whether there was a hidden price to pay for eating the big ugly tomatoes. We came home laden with fruit, and Rob, a culinary genius, made peach cobbler for dessert.

That evening, my sister and I took a drive out to Thomasville. This was where her daddy, our father, had died and was buried. As she told me about her life, she showed me the houses they had lived in – houses that Eugene himself had built with his own hands. He was a hard worker. She showed me the first house they had lived in when the family had moved back from Florida, and she talked about the shock of waking up to snow on the ground the day after they had arrived. They had no warm clothes because they hadn't needed them before, living by the warm ocean on the Florida coast. She drove us past the house where he had been shot and killed. It was an unassuming small brick bungalow with a pick-up truck parked in the driveway. The hood was up. A man working on the truck scowled at us as we drove slowly by, probably thinking we were casing the joint. He didn't look too impressed as we turned the van around and drove slowly back again. I was trying not to stare at the house, but I wanted to see it.

We went to the cemetery to visit Eugene's grave. Two daughters who had never known the other even existed. Jean said, "I never thought I'd be back here with an Englishwoman." We sat on the grass at his grave and talked. It was a peaceful place. The church, up over the hill from the gravesite, was huge; it was not the original building that had been there when Eugene had met with Pastor Greene, and God, on that day he was born again. That building had burned down years before and had been replaced by the massive red brick structure that stands there today. Jean hadn't been to the church in years. It had been only the previous August that she had finally come to Eugene's gravesite, to sit and reflect, and make peace with her father. She told me that Pastor Greene had passed away some time ago. We talked for hours. There was a man walking his dogs around the pathway that circled the acres of cemetery. On his third circuit, we noticed that he was looking at us rather strangely, no doubt wondering what we two middle-aged women could be doing, sitting on the grass amongst the gravestones for hours on end. We laughed. It was a good and healing time for me. I had never imagined in my wildest dreams that I would be able to see where my father was buried, let alone sit in the cool of the evening at his grave with a sister I never knew existed, and talk about his life. The good and the bad, the tears and the laughter; I wouldn't have missed that for the world.

Later that evening back at the house, Jean handed me Eugene's leather-bound Bible, and the little New Testament he had carried everywhere with him during those years when he had turned away from alcohol. The Bible is a Scofield, with his name embossed in gold on the soft hide cover. It's a beautiful thing, but the dog-eared little New Testament was almost a part of Eugene himself. He carried it everywhere in his shirt pocket, and it's full of little notes that he wrote on the pages, his handwriting right there to see, just like Edith's on her payment slips in my adoption file. There were tags on the pages so that he could turn to his favourite passages quickly. There are still little hand-out cards in there printed with, "Jesus Loves You". He kept them there to give out to people he met and talked to. I imagined I could still feel him and touch him through the pages of that little book. He had turned those pages, written those notes, read those words. It brought him to life.

Eugene's parents, brothers and sisters had wanted him to be buried with that New Testament in his hands, but Jean and her mama Louisa didn't think it would be right. He hadn't been that same person when he died, and it was a precious reminder to those left behind of the man he had once been. Jean had taken the book from his hands as he lay in the casket at the funeral home, and she replaced it with a yellow rose, her favourite flower. And that is how he was buried. His family never knew.

11

Part of the Family

The next morning Jean was off to work again, just for a few hours, and Rob was gone somewhere for the morning. I didn't mind, I could get my first cup of coffee and sit on the shady deck, relaxing. It was good to have that time. Today I would be meeting Carla, Jean's older sister. I wasn't sure exactly what to expect. Jean had told me some things about Carla, but I had the feeling I had to read between the lines of what she had told me. Carla was loud, she said. And unreliable sometimes; Carla would say she was going to do things and then not do them, make promises and then not follow through. "You'll understand when you meet her," she had said. "If she turns up." I was intrigued.

Carla did turn up, but later than I had expected her. I was sitting on the deck when she arrived, listening to the birds singing, and I heard her coming long before I saw her. The French doors opened, and there she was, larger than life, greeting me with wide open arms and a giant bear hug. My first thought as she enveloped me was that she had so much hair! Wild and frizzy and thick and long, and such a sweet face. She certainly was a large lady with a large personality and a large voice. Everything about her was, well – large. She didn't look at all like the little girl in the photograph. She didn't look like Jean, either. She sat, and we talked. Or Carla talked, anyway. She had a loud and lazy slow way of talking, musing on the words she chose. She told me, "There ain't such a thing as a half-sister, you're either a sister or you ain't. And you're Jean's sister, and that makes you my sister, too."

She told me about growing up with Eugene as a father. Carla had grown up in Florida, by the sea. She had loved it there. Eugene had moved her and Louisa to Florida soon after they had married. Carla was just a little girl then, and Jean hadn't yet been born. Eugene worked hard, but he drank hard, too. He was mean, and he didn't like Carla, so he was especially mean to her. Carla was smart. She was a Straight-A student, and a gifted violinist. She was musical. I couldn't equate what I was hearing with the woman sitting across the table from me. She worked for a trucking company, spoke the language of truckers peppered with the profanities of truckers. What had happened to that little girl to change her so much?

Eugene had moved the family to small town North Carolina when Carla was sixteen. It was a culture shock to all of them, but for Carla it was life changing. She had been a successful and popular student, an accomplished musician; she played in an orchestra, she had good friends and good prospects. It looked like her life was mapped out. She knew where she wanted to go in life, and she was on her way. And then, the move. It took her away from everything and everybody she knew. She was dumped into a little "podunk" town (her own words, podunk being slang for anywhere that's nowhere worth being); into a small-minded podunk school filled with students suspicious of outsiders. It may as well have been a million miles away from the sophisticated metropolitan worldly-wise environment she was accustomed to. Carla couldn't handle it. She had a breakdown, she turned to drugs, she got caught up in bad relationships, she had bad trips. She has never recovered. Looking at her as she spoke,

I wondered who she might have become had her life not taken that turn. It was really painful to see the wasted potential in this big-hearted person.

But anyway, here she was, larger and louder than life itself, telling me that she understood why I needed to find out who I was. She had looked for and found her own biological father when she was twenty five. She hadn't wanted to have a continuing relationship with him, she had just wanted to see him. She had done that; it had been enough for her. She was forthright. I decided I liked Carla a lot.

Dean came home and the three of us sat around talking on the deck. Carla talked about the night Eugene had died. She hadn't been at the house when it happened; she had her own place by then so what she knew was only what she had been told by her mama. Carrie, who was only thirteen years old, had been there and had seen everything. Her mama was an angel, Carla said. That's exactly how Dean had described her, too. Carla said Louisa had been her best friend. After the shooting, Carla had lived with her until she died, and she still lived in Mama's old townhouse. We passed the afternoon listening to Carla's memories.

Rob came home and made "Continental Chicken" – I wasn't sure exactly what was continental about it, but it looked and smelled delicious. Jean arrived home from work at the hospital, looking hot and tired in her nursing scrubs. "I'm going to shower," she said, pulling the band from her ponytail and shaking her hair loose. She emerged from the shower a little later looking cool and refreshed, and we ate supper on the deck. It seemed like they lived outdoors here, and I loved it. It was still 100 degrees in the late afternoon sun, but it was pleasant and cool in the shade of the big trees. I was beginning to feel settled.

Later, Jean and I sat with Carla and we went through the

handwritten family tree I had begun to draw up back in England. The Gallaghers and the Russells of North Carolina both traced back to Scotland in the fifteen hundreds, to the Western Isles. We had solid Scottish roots. We talked about the Russells – Louisa had been a Russell, but so had Eugene's mother, so Louisa and Eugene had been second cousins. It was complicated and we were all related and cross related to the Russells. Mama Russell as she was called, Louisa's mother, was a much-loved legend on both sides of the family. Everybody had loved her. I showed them photographs of Edith which I had brought with me, and Sandra and her daughter Jean. A melange of different mothers and fathers, but we laughed as three sisters together, and I started to feel like I had really come home, after more than fifty years away. It was a strange feeling indeed.

RibFest was in town at nearby Winston-Salem so the next day we went - Jean, Carla and I - because it was apparently an experience not to be missed. They were not joking! I had seen nothing like this before. There was a car show, live music, lots of noise and crowds of people just having fun. Vendors with names like Pigfoot, Sergeant Oinks and Texas Thunder had brightly coloured barbecue stands and were cooking up piles of ribs in smokers and on grills, dry-rubbed with secret spice recipes and then slathered in even more secret barbecue sauces. They were competing for awards like Grand Champion and People's Choice. It was an absolute assault on the culinary senses, and not only ribs but chicken, different kinds of slaw, "blooming onions", funnel cakes, elephant ears (no not real ones), deep fried killer-hot jalapeno peppers, deep fried butter, Twinkies, Snickers Bars, Oreos – you name it, they deep fried it and people ate it. Carla bought a funnel cake for us to share, it was as big as a platter and dusted in icing sugar. They certainly know how to eat in the South.

I had been making plans to stay with Martha for a few days the following week and spend some time with her and Jolene. Originally I had intended to stay with Jolene, but she lived in a small mobile home and was short on space, whereas Martha and her husband lived in a larger house and so they had offered to put me up. The plan was to take a drive out to Robeson County to see the town of their childhood, Red Springs, where the Gallagher children had grown up. I wanted to see where Eugene had lived, see the streets he had walked down, and the store where he had bought his can of Mountain Dew every day. I was apprehensive about going to Martha's after what had happened before I came, and I wasn't too sure how truly welcome I was going to be. Jean suggested we take a trip to the Blue Ridge Mountains for a few days first, so that I could decompress, relax and we could get to know each other better. It was a perfect idea.

And so I became a regular tourist. We planned our trip over breakfast the next morning. Grits and eggs, with country ham. Grits, a quintessentially Southern comfort food, and breakfast would not be the same without them, but this was my first experience. The word conjures up small hard pieces of gravely corn getting caught up in teeth, a little bit like that awful experience of coffee grounds washing into your mouth at the end of the cup. I wasn't sure what to expect, but when my sister brought out a steaming bowl of what looked like a smooth creamy porridge and proceeded to put butter on it, I thought I'd give it a try. I discovered that grits were wonderful. I now understood why Captain John Smith had been so captivated in 1607 by that band of Natives, who greeted him with bowls of hominy grits as he stepped wearily ashore in what later became known as Virginia. Grits have a long history in the South and are an ingrained part of the culture. No pun intended.

The innocuous-sounding country ham, cured and sometimes smoked, is served in thick slices with red eye gravy. This delightful concoction of a sauce is made with the drippings from the ham mixed with black coffee. It sounds awful but is incredibly tasty. They call it red eye because when it's poured into a round bowl, the meaty bits and the coffee sink to the bottom, leaving a layer of grease floating on the top and it gives the appearance of a human eye, with the iris looking red. Well so they say. The ham is sometimes placed in a buttered split "biscuit" – a tender, soft and flaky savoury type of scone. Country ham is truly an American culinary masterpiece. European hams are world renowned; the Italians have Prosciutto and Parma, the Spanish have Serrano and Jamon, and the French the wonderful Jambon de Bayonne. But these American hams would rival the individuality and quality of some of Europe's finest. Hams are produced by small farms in Kentucky, Tennessee, North Carolina and Virginia, each to their own family recipe passed down through generations. Cured with brown sugar, honey, salt and spices, using the same natural processes employed by the early colonists, the finished product is as unique as the producers themselves. An untapped and little-known treasure outside of the Southern States.

We were off to the famous Blue Ridge Mountains. We packed up the van and headed west along the freeway, towards the Blue Ridge Parkway for three days of exploring the hazy, smoky blue mountains. This is Daniel Boone country; old settlers' cabins, the imposing Moses Cone House which is a masterpiece of Victorian neocolonial architecture, set up high on a mountain top. Small Appalachian towns and wineries, with thunderstorms rolling through the scenic valleys. This trip was just what the doctor ordered, and by the time we returned to my sister's home I felt almost ready to face what was going to be a challenge for me, and certainly a challenge for my father's sisters.

Ominously, there were storms all that preceding night, and I couldn't sleep with all the crashing and booming outside. In the morning I phoned Martha to arrange a meeting place and time. It felt a bit like a spy hand-over from the Cold War and I briefly wondered whether I should look for a long bridge for the drop-off point; an isolated spot for me to get slowly out of the car, walk across No Man's Land and get into another waiting vehicle - and the unknown - on the far side of the bridge. I was being cynical pf course, but Martha and Jean most definitely weren't ready to meet in person, so Rob drove me to the appointed place alone. Not a bridge, but in typically American fashion, a shopping mall. Dean had tried to convince me to take his gun with me. He told me in no uncertain terms that these were bad people, and I needed to be careful. I declined the gun offer, at first thinking he must have been joking, but he was very serious. This went some way towards demonstrating the level of distrust and misunderstanding that had grown between the two sides of the family over the thirty or so years that had passed since Louisa had killed Eugene. After I had left Rob and the van and walked across the parking lot to the waiting car, Martha and her husband got out and greeted me. There were no hugs, but more formal handshakes. It felt a little strange. We went to a restaurant in the mall. The place was called Apex, and the thunderstorm had followed us all the way there. I wondered again if it were an omen.

We were joined at the restaurant by Martha's son James, his wife and their two little girls. We talked while we ate. It was all a little strange. I remember thinking that James' wife seemed quite uptight and I couldn't figure out why. The little girls were sweet, quite close in age and obviously the apple of their grandpa's eye. I sat next to Martha and watched her nervously smoothing, folding and rolling the table napkin over and over. It was mesmerising. She had a certain pattern that she followed, and once folded and rolled, it was undone, smoothed flat and the whole process started again. She caught me watching her, and said, "If you're a true Gallagher, you'll always have two napkins." Then she laughed and told me how she also sorts M & M candies into flavours and colours. Definitely OCD, I thought to myself. Martha was much smaller than I'd imagined, in fact she was tiny, and she was very sweet to me. I couldn't relate what I saw in front of me to the harsh, angry words she had messaged me only the week before. I decided to file that whole episode away under Mishaps and enjoy the time I had to spend with my aunt.

12

AUNT MARTHA

In the car driving back to Fayetteville, Martha had asked me about my birth mother and the adoption. I felt she was testing the waters. Then, when she felt confident, she told me what had happened to spark the sudden change in her and Jolene's attitude the week before. The four sisters, Martha, Jolene, Ruby and Roseanne, had gotten together – a meeting of The Sisterhood had been called - after Ruby had received the letter Jean had written to her; pouring out her heart and asking if the two of us could visit her while I was over in America. Ruby had shown her sisters the letter. There followed a discussion, and the outcome of this was that it was all too painful for them to deal with. Even after 30 years, they could not revisit what had happened in their family. On that day they had all been of one mind, and the collective decision was made to have nothing further to do with either me or Jean.

I feel it says a lot about who are the more dominant and the more submissive personalities in the sisterhood. I recalled what Roseanne had said about Ruby being stubborn and strong minded, and the reticence of the others to counter what she said. Martha told me she had gone to bed that night feeling uncomfortable about the decision. She had convinced herself that it must be the right decision, after all they had been in agreement at the time and it had made sense to her then, so it could surely not be wrong.

Martha is a devout Southern Baptist and the next morning, as is her daily habit, she had risen early for her "quiet time" which she spent meditating and reading her Bible. She had opened her Bible and had been struck right away by a verse on the page. It was 2 Corinthians 1:17, "You may be asking why I changed my plan. Do you think I make my plans carelessly? Do you think I am like people of the world who say "Yes" when they really mean "No"?" It pricked Martha's conscience. She had reflected on this for a while, then closed her Bible, showered, dressed and gone off to work, still feeling troubled in her spirit.

At her desk in her office she had switched on her computer and opened her first email. It was from a Christian friend who had felt compelled to share a Bible verse with her. When she opened the email, it was the same verse she had read at home. Feeling more than a little unsettled, she had moved on to her next email. It was the daily motivational message that all the staff where she worked received. It was about decision-making. Martha had shut off her computer and gone home.

When she got home, she decided to email Jolene and tell her she was convinced they had made the wrong decision. But there was already a message in her inbox from Jolene, asking her whether she thought they had made the wrong decision. She phoned Jolene and told her she had made up her mind to see me and that she knew it had been wrong to shut me out. They arranged to meet for lunch to talk and compare notes. Jolene had independently reached the same conclusion, but they were afraid by now that I would want nothing to do with them, after what had already been said to me in haste, and I believe out of fear. I was a person who could dredge up the unwanted and deeply buried past. One look at me in the flesh could bring everything back because there was no doubt that I bore a striking physical resemblance to their long dead brother.

After they had met and agreed that they would like to meet with me after all, Jolene had contacted my daughter with the news that they had changed their minds. So after all that, here I was in North Carolina with Martha, the aunt I almost never met.

Martha lives in a simple single storey home on a quiet residential street in Fayetteville, surrounded by similarly unassuming suburban homes. Her husband Don drives a Ford pickup truck and Martha drives a big Ford Crown Victoria sedan. Martha and Don are Ford people. I am discovering that people are either Ford people or Chevy people, and you can't mix and match. I loved Martha's car. It was new, huge and extremely comfortable. It had air conditioning, which I quickly found out was an absolute necessity with the hot and humid North Carolina days. Not all cars had air conditioning back in England, but then it rarely gets that hot. We went for a "spin-around" in the car the next day, just the two of us, while Don was off at work. Don is a schoolteacher, which is his second career. He is a retired military man, and he and Martha have travelled and lived all over America with his military postings. Don is Martha's second husband. They have been settled in this house, which they built, for quite a few years. Don teaches Fifth Grade at a junior school, and the kids all love him. He has a gruff exterior but a heart of pure gold; he gives them the solid boundaries and the structure which many do not have at home. It is clear he loves his job. I realised very quickly that he provides Martha with that same much-needed stability and structure – she needs it, she is sweet and kind, but vague and distant, obsessive compulsive and quite phobic. There's a lot going on with her. I wondered if she could manage without that solid kind man guiding her and providing such regimented stability.

Martha and I drove in her fabulous new Ford to downtown Fayetteville. It was a cool and beautiful oasis in the heat, with tree lined streets, cafes and restaurants. It feels almost European. We went to her office for a panoramic view over the City. We had a soda in a bar, and then went to see the slipway on the Cape Fear River, where she and Don launch their boat and spend the day fishing for catfish and whatever else they can hook. The paddleboat steamers and the big boats would come all the way up from Wilmington once, she told me. They would stop right there at Campbelltown Landing. It must have taken days to get up the river from the coast, and it was hard to imagine that quiet and tranquil spot as a busy dock.

Martha told me about her family. She had been married before, and her three boys were adult sons of that first marriage. Don had been married before too, and had grown-up daughters living elsewhere. I had met James, Martha's youngest son, at the restaurant in Apex with his wife and two young daughters. James is the only one of the three with a career. She proudly tells me that he has made it in life; his wife is a professional too, and they epitomise the successful middle-class American family. They have a nice house in a nice neighbourhood, and a very nice life. James, she tells me, is a lot like his father in many ways. "But not all." This sounded quite cryptic. "I have struggled with how much to tell the boys about their father, but you can't protect them forever," she says. I wonder what she means. James has done some research on the family, she tells me, although she doesn't elaborate. Much later, I was to find out what she was alluding to and I fervently hoped that James was not at all like his father.

Jessie is her middle son, always in trouble, living life on

the edge; into drugs and hanging out with his drug addict friends. Martha is quite open with me about all this, which I find a little disconcerting. She won't bail him out again, she tells me. As she talks about Jessie and his lifestyle I am reminded of Merle, my father's brother. Jessie has a teenage daughter who lives in Texas with her mother. Her mother, Martha tells me, is a prostitute and a drug addict. It doesn't sound good.

And then there's her youngest son Eugene, who I presume is named after my biological father. She says Eugene is childlike. "Acts like a fourteen-year-old and cannot take care of himself. He wouldn't want to meet you, because he hates the police. He's been in some trouble," she explains. Eugene lives in a mobile home outside of town. She and Don have recently set him up there; they bought the trailer, fixed it up and made it a home for him. I don't want to push Martha to elaborate, but she tells me anyway.

Eugene had recently been released from prison. He had been incarcerated for rather a long time. Before his troubles, he had been staying with Martha and Don when early one morning the police had raided their house. They had taken away some videos which Eugene had coincidentally been going to get rid of the next day. She said he had told her he wanted to get out of "whatever he had been into". She didn't want to say the actual words, child pornography. But it was all too late for Eugene to "get out". He had been arrested on the spot and charged. There had been a trial and the Judge had found him guilty and sent him to prison. He had done his time, but his associate in crime was still inside, serving twenty five years for his part in making and distributing child pornography. Later I read the court transcripts online because they're available to the general public in North Carolina, as are the names and full details of sex offenders. Yes, Eugene was on that list. He and his sidekick had been making films with children and Eugene had a starring role. I was glad that he hadn't wanted to meet me. I don't think I would have wanted to meet him, either.

How do you measure the depth of a mother's love? It seemed as if Martha had never doubted Eugene's story or stopped believing in him, probably because to face something like that about your child would be soul destroying. She had gone to court most days to support him but the experience of that trial must have almost killed her. My heart went out to her. She told me she had gone to the pastor at her church for emotional support and had been turned away because of the nature of her son's crime. In a way I could understand that, but it wasn't her fault that her son did what he did, and although she was clearly still very much in denial, she would have needed help to get through that awful time and she didn't get it from her church. I wondered where the Southern Baptist Jesus was in the decision to turn her away.

It had been an emotional day for both of us, and we needed some time to chill out. We finished up our day with a steak dinner in the company of Jolene and her husband Lorne, at the Lonestar Restaurant. The best steaks in town, I was told, and I was not disappointed with the steaks, or the company. This was my first meeting with Jolene. I had been so looking forward to meeting her: she was the one I had found first, the lady who wears her heart on her sleeve, says what she thinks, and thinks afterwards about what she has said. I was thankful again that it had been Jolene I had found that night after getting back home from Barnardo's. If it had been one of the others, I am not sure any of this would have happened. And her husband Lorne, the man in the wedding photograph with the kind face, a big bear of a man in the flesh, but soft spoken and "easy-tempered" as Jolene describes him. He keeps her calm, she says. He's a Chevy man with a big black pick-up truck, which is his pride and joy. He even has a tattoo which matches a sticker on his truck. We spent a wonderful evening, laughing and sharing happy stories from our lives. Tomorrow we would go to Robeson County, Martha, Jolene and I. They would show me where the Gallagher family had lived, and where they and my father had grown up. I was looking forward to it immensely.

13

Roots and Swamps

Back Swamp. What a great name for a place, conjuring up images of deep, still, stagnant water, dangling tendrils of dark green vines, strange sounds made by unseen creatures and the beating wings of large flying insects. "It's where I was born," Martha said, "Back Swamp. It's right there on my birth certificate." I had visions of my paternal grandmother giving birth to her daughter in this remote alien place. I could not imagine anyone giving birth by choice here. Perhaps they had been on a family picnic in the countryside for the day and she had gone into labour unexpectedly.

But of course, Back Swamp is an old settlement. Not a municipality, not a town, not anything as grand even as a village. Today it's just a collection of ragtag tumbledown shacks strung out along a dirt road. True, there was a swamp there, in fact it was almost the only thing that was there. Except the cemetery.

For some reason best known to them, this was where our Gallagher ancestors had chosen to settle when they first came to North Carolina. There's nothing now to suggest what made this the right place for them to settle and build their houses, their church, their schoolhouse, and to raise their families. But this is where the Gallaghers had settled after arriving from Scotland some time in the 1700's.

Somewhere in the undergrowth there is a long-abandoned cemetery with ancient headstones belonging to long dead Gallaghers. Barnabas Gallagher is buried there; Barnabas who, as family legend has it, killed one of his own children with an axe. I am finding out some disturbing things about this family. We didn't go looking for the cemetery. Back Swamp was a strange place, not what I had expected, although with a name like Back Swamp who would know what to expect? So after a photograph by the Back Swamp road sign to say for posterity that we had been there, we moved on.

In the cool of the air-conditioned car with Martha and Jolene, we drove past tobacco fields where they had worked with their mama as children, while their daddy had toiled in the cotton mill. Jolene described how they had been taught to bundle the tobacco leaves together, then tied them and hung them upside down on long poles for drying in the sheds. There was a technique to it. It had been hot, hard work, but it was what they had all done to survive. Everybody played their part in supporting the family. These days, the tobacco fields have largely been replaced with fields of maize and hemp, and those that remain are harvested with machinery. It made me wonder what the people there did for a living now. Working in the fields was hard, but it gave the families a kind of self pride and a sense of achievement. What they had was not much, but it was gained honestly by hard work.

We pulled up beside what looked to me like an ordinary piece of scrubby land; dry and sandy with sparse vegetation and a few spindly trees dotted here and there. Jolene said, "Your daddy chased me down this road for two miles one day when I made him mad." She pointed across the field, "Our house was right there," she said, "In the pecan trees. We rented it off a man who had cows." There was nothing left there now to show for her memories; no sign of the house but the pecan trees were still there. The family had moved into the nearby town of Red Springs after leaving that house.

Robeson County, where the family grew up, is the largest county in North Carolina. The terrain varies from sand hills to numerous small swamps and backwaters, interspersed with small towns dotted all around the countryside. The towns have a dusty old-time look to them, full of the history of grander days long since gone. There are huge antebellum mansions, now looking a little weary, along wide tree-lined streets; peeling paint on old boarding houses, creeping undergrowth taking back the once manicured gardens. Red Springs is such a town. Coming into town we drove past a ramshackle, white-boarded Mexican restaurant, festooned with brightly coloured lanterns and garish signs announcing "Taqueria" or taco shop. Martha told me that, back when they were living here, this used to be the general store that Eugene had walked to every day to get his can of Mountain Dew. We drove past a large modern red brick building, the United Pentecostal Church, announcing "Welcome to the Up-Church of Red Springs, Where God is Lifting People Up! Martha told me that the church had been rebuilt after a tornado which had swept through and devastated the town in 1984. One of my cousins, a little girl named Tanika, had been killed in that church during the tornado. She was there with her older brother Bobby for the Wednesday evening Bible Study when the church took a direct hit. Tanika was just two years old.

Tanika and Bobby, along with their older sister Gina were part Lumbee. Uncle Robert, Eugene's brother who died of cancer, had married a Lumbee woman, Wilma Lee. The Lumbee people are an interesting tribe of Indigenous people little known outside of North Carolina. Their origins are uncertain, and they are distinguished from other indigenous peoples in the United States by the fact that they are not federally recognised as a Native American Tribe. They do not benefit financially from federal funding, even though they are the largest tribe east of the Mississippi River. Their population is still centred on the Lumber River, a dark, swampy twisting waterway, as it was in the 18th Century when their existence was first documented.

Their origins are mysterious. It is thought that they may be descendants of the Tuscarora people who were encountered by the first settlers, but then the Lumbee people have many different physical traits from the Tuscarora. Some are dark skinned with features reminiscent of black African slaves, but then there are some with red hair and freckles, and some are fair skinned. Early records refer to the Lumbee as "mulatto" which was a word commonly used to describe mixed race people.

Their strangely European way of life was unusual in the 1700's when later settlers rediscovered them. They were already practising Christianity, they spoke the English language and were building European-style houses. They utilised recognisable European farming methods. One school of thought is that the Lumbee people are descendants of the Lost Colony of Roanoke; these were early coastal settlers who established a colony on Roanoke Island in the 1587 but then disappeared without trace before 1590, leaving only a carving in a tree as a clue: the word Croataon. This is believed to refer to the Croatan Indians, a friendly tribe with whom they had established ties, but the significance of the carving is still not known. What happened to those settlers is a mystery. The earliest documented Lumbee family names certainly include the last names of some of the lost colonists, but this remains a contentious theory. In any case, the Lumbee population today is thriving; they are the ninth largest indigenous tribe in North America, and they are a very proud and independent people.

Nonetheless, it would not have been socially acceptable for Robert, a young white man, to marry a Lumbee woman and there is no doubt that he would have faced opposition from within his family. While I was visiting North Carolina I saw overt evidence of racism, even within the Gallagher family. Gina, my part Lumbee cousin, was getting married during the time I was staying with my sister Jean, and several members of the Gallagher family had been invited to the wedding. The only people to attend were Martha and Don, and this was kept quiet, as it would still be frowned upon for upstanding white people to attend a Lumbee wedding. Racism is still alive and well in the South. As a footnote, I was also told that Wilma Lee had been seriously injured when Robert had driven his car off the road while steaming drunk. I don't know what happened to her after that, but I do believe she was another female victim of the hard-drinking and violent Gallagher men.

Moving on with the day, our next stop was at the Flora MacDonald College. This used to be a private all-women's school located in the very heart of the town of Red Springs. Set in ten acres of pleasant gardens, and with its own small swamp, this place had been Red Spring's claim to fame back in the early 1900's. It was certainly grand in its day, yet it now seemed out of place in the rundown town. The main building is red brick and has towering white pillars giving it a grandiose air. The large heavy wooden doors were unlocked so we went inside. The interior of the massive conservatory hall was lined with rich wood panelling and the old wooden trestle dining tables were still set out as if waiting for supper to be served. Again, the peeling paint on the window frames spoke of the grander days of the past. The school's roots go back to the days of the settling Scots, when the young girls were taught traditional Scottish folk dances and wore pretty Highland costumes.

Flora MacDonald, the Scottish heroine, is famous for helping Bonnie Prince Charlie escape from Scotland after his defeat at the bloody battle of Culloden. Disguised as Flora's maid "Betty Burke", the Young Pretender Prince had made the journey by rowing boat from Uist to the Isle of Skye with Flora, who had then helped him escape to France. She had been imprisoned in Oban for her part in helping the Prince escape but had later married her fiancé Allan MacDonald and emigrated to North Carolina. Flora was a legend amongst the Scottish population there, but after the American War of Independence during which her husband and one of her sons was imprisoned, she returned to her roots in Scotland where she died in 1790. She is buried there, in Kilmuir, with a sheet which the Prince had slept in as her shroud. The original headstone slate from her monument has now been placed in the gardens at the Flora MacDonald College, over the graves of two of her sons who are interred there. It is a fittingly peaceful spot.

Almost every American town has a dividing line of railway tracks running down through the middle. Generally, the houses to the west of the tracks are nicer than those on the east side, although I don't know why that should be, but hence the saying, "from the wrong side of the tracks". As we drove past an overgrown plot of land on the not-so-salubrious east side of Red Springs, Jolene suddenly said from the back seat, "That's where the red house used to be." We stopped. The red house was no longer there – it was an empty plot of land, but this was the house they had first lived in when they moved into town from the house in the pecan trees. She remembered the red house being full of cockroaches when they had lived there, before they had moved across the street to a small wooden sided single storey house which was just a little nicer, and that house was still standing for me to see. It didn't look big enough to have housed the Gallagher family with all those children, but that's where they had lived. Mama cooked in the hot kitchen, fatback with collard greens for supper. There were children playing in the yard that day we visited, and the pecan tree that Jolene remembered was still standing. Eugene had been long gone to the Air Force before they had moved into that house, but it was where Jolene and Martha, the younger sisters, had the most memories of growing up. They had shared a room and shared the same bed – they had to - until Martha finally moved out when she got married. And it was the stories they told of what had happened in that house that were to stay with me long after my trip to North Carolina was over.

"Daddy, don't hit me…PLEASE!" Martha would cry, as Eugene Senior lined the children up and beat them, one by one. And when Martha sobbed, he would laugh at her, and she knew he would tell everyone he knew that all she ever did was cry. One day, the bedroom door had blown shut in the breeze and Jolene, never one to give up easily, told me how he had blamed her for slamming the door and had beaten her with a belt for forty-five minutes trying to make her cry. She told me that he had literally had to stop because he got too tired to hit her anymore. She did not cry; she had learned the lesson from Martha well.

On car journeys the children would sit in the back seat, hands tucked in, knees turned sideways, too scared to move. If they should accidentally touch the back of their daddy's car seat with hands or knees, he would hit the brakes, stop the car and turn around and slap them all hard. He wouldn't stop for toilet breaks. The girls would plead, "Please Mama, make Daddy stop!" But Mama would never say a word to him because she was scared of him too. Once, he had left

Jolene behind after stopping to refuel the car. She had run to the toilet, desperate, but had taken too long. He had filled up the car, paid for the gas and driven off by the time she had come out of the washroom. She was six years old and he just left her there. She had panicked. Forty minutes later he had come back to collect her and had given her another beating.

Jolene told me how he had abused their mother. He had chased her around the yard of that little house with a rifle, taking aim and trying to shoot her until she had run off and hidden in the cornfields. Jolene and Martha, terrified, had hidden under the house in the dirt with the dogs until Mama had come home.

Jolene remembers her daddy losing his temper and hitting her mama across the head with a kitchen chair, splitting her head open. There was blood everywhere and Mama was acting dazed. The doctor was called to patch her up but, as Jolene said, the men stuck together. The doctor looked at Mama lying on the bed, bleeding and bruised. "She's just crazy," the doctor had said, "There's nothing else wrong with her."

Those poor women, my two aunts; my father's sisters, broke my heart that day. They spoke of these terrible events from their past in such a matter-of-fact way. No emotions, no tears for what had happened to them or their mama. Just plain, factual accounts of terrible events. That had been their life. As the saying goes, the apple doesn't fall far from the tree. Little wonder my father had been so abusive to Louisa and his daughters; he had learned his lessons well from his own father. My sister Jean had told me how he would never stop the car on their journeys from Florida to Red Springs when they came to visit. He would stop only for gas, never for the washroom. And he would slap their legs hard if they moved in the back seat, just like his own father had done to him.

The legacy that Eugene Senior left behind is plain to see; Jolene suffers panic attacks and is fearful to go on long journeys in the car. I had no idea at the time that it had been so difficult for her that day to even get into the car with Martha and me, and then drive all the way to Red Springs. She had been afraid herself to get behind the wheel and drive us that day in case she would have a panic attack and embarrass herself. Martha is obsessive compulsive; everything has to be "just so". Of course it does, because it had to then, or there would be a beating. Martha doesn't like loud noises. No wonder. And she's afraid of insects, as would I be, had I grown up in a house full of cockroaches. I hadn't had the opportunity to meet Belle, Roseanne, Ruby or Merle but there was no doubt in my mind that they would carry the scars of their upbringing in their behaviour, too. But for all that, they professed to love their father despite the damage he did to them all. "He was a hard man, but fair," Jolene said. That day I learned a lot about my family history, and I wondered if perhaps I had learned more than I had wanted to.

Despite the awful revelations of that day, I had really enjoyed getting to know my two aunts and was grateful that they had decided to go ahead and meet with me after all. We ended the day with an all-you-can eat buffet at a restaurant serving a selection of classic Southern foods - mostly deep fried - including catfish, chicken gizzards (which I was led to believe are a kind of delicacy) and yes, fatback with collard greens. I was determined to try as many different dishes as I could, and I may have overdone things because I had the worst heartburn of my life back at Martha's that night. Still, it was worth it.

I spent the next day relaxing with Jolene and Lorne at their mobile home, being regaled with stories of a giant alligator which was supposedly living in a small pond at the end of their road, and which would appear without warning on the front lawns to terrorise the residents. Cats and small dogs had disappeared quite regularly. No-one had been able to capture the beast despite the best efforts of the local pest control. There were also snakes to be careful of, most notably Copperheads, which were quite deadly and had a penchant for getting into the mobile homes and hiding behind kitchen appliances. Getting back to England with its benign wildlife was starting to seem more attractive.

The next day I was going to be handed back over to Jean and her family. The plan was to spend a few days at the legendary Myrtle Beach for a chance to relax before catching my flight back to England. The handover from one side of the family back to the other was due to take place outside a Walmart store at a shopping mall near Lumberton. This turned out to be one of the high points not only of the trip, but of the entire story of my adoption search. It was a hot sunny day, and Jolene and Lorne had driven me to the mall in Lorne's giant black pick-up truck. Jean and Rob were waiting in the van when we pulled in. it was such a privilege for me to witness my sister Jean and my aunt Jolene greet each other after being estranged for more than thirty years. They looked at each other, then they hugged and cried, and they both agreed that it was thirty years needlessly spent apart. The men shook hands, as men do. It had been agreed that this meeting would happen before we had set off that morning. I suspected Rob was behind it and had coached Jean through it. Martha wasn't ready to meet Jean, so she stayed at home and we had said our goodbyes there. But Jolene, big hearted and ready to admit things may not have been done right all those years ago, was ready to forgive and ready to reconcile. It was such a wonderful moment, and I realised then that although I had always thought my adoption journey was all about me finding out who I was and where my place was in the world, that it was also very much about them. If I hadn't taken the plunge and begun my search, they may never have reconciled or had the chance to begin to heal from the past. It was a very powerful and humbling moment.

14

Crocodiles and Goodbye Tears

On Friday morning at Myrtle Beach, I awoke to the sound of a loud klaxon, sirens wailing and people shouting. It was loud, even from the lofty heights of the Cherry Grove Resort tower and our suite on the fourteenth floor high above the beach. As I shook off the last vestiges of sleep, I wondered if I had been transported somehow back to wartime London and the blitz. The sirens were loud enough. I threw off the bedcovers and walked across to the patio doors. I pulled open the heavy curtains, fumbled around for the door catch and slid the door open. The wall of heat hit me as I tumbled out onto the balcony, blinking in the bright sunlight of the South Carolina coast.

Below me, down on the beach, there was a lot of excited shouting; a crowd of people gathered by the wooden struts of the pier reaching out into the ocean, fingers pointing at what looked to me like a large inert log floating sideways along out in the water. The lifeguards were down from their umbrella-shaded, white-painted watchtowers, moving people back from the water's edge, shouting at bathers to get out of the water NOW! It was like Baywatch, happening right before my eyes. I was almost expecting to see David Hasselhoff come sprinting up the beach. Jean joined me on the balcony. "It must be a shark, sis," she said. It didn't look like a shark to me, but I wasn't sure what it was.

We threw on our bathing suits, stepped into our sandals, summoned the elevator, and then walked out onto the beach. By this time, the crowd and the floating log had moved with the current well down from the pier. We walked across the already hot sand. It was early morning, but the air was already warm and there were lots of people out catching the rays, no doubt before the summer sun got too hot to bear. Mad dogs and Englishmen, I thought. These were sensible beachgoers.

We started working our way through the crowd. "Step back from the water, ma'am," a tanned lifeguard said to a middle-aged, scantily clad woman who was standing several feet out in the surf. She stepped back and I asked her what all the fuss was about. "It's a gator," she said. A gator? An alligator? In the ocean? "Naw," said Jean in her Southern accent, "Can't be. That's just a bit of seaweed." But of course, seaweed doesn't trigger a turnout by the emergency services; the inert log was indeed a fairly large reptile of the alligator family, floating unconcerned, bobbing eyeballs above the surf, keeping a lazy watch on the excited group of humans as they matched its progress along the shoreline. It wasn't actually an alligator, it was a sea crocodile and yes indeed, they live quite happily in salt water and fresh. Who knew?

People were starting to venture back into the water behind us on the now-safe far side of the pier, as we moved further down the beach. We walked along slowly with the crowd, following the bobbing reptile, admiring the tans of the bikini-clad girls as they strolled along in front of us. It wouldn't be too hard to get a fabulous natural tan here, after all; a yearly average of over two hundred full days of sun would see to that. I shuddered to think of the skin damage caused by that much sun exposure. Sunscreen would not be optional. My sister and I decided we would buy ourselves a beach house one day and live out our lives alternately sunning ourselves on the sandy beach and cooling ourselves off in the wonderful warm Atlantic. Croc-free days only, of course.

I had really needed the time to relax after the raw emotions of the past two weeks, and Jean had known that. What a perfect idea to end my visit with this beach break. It all went too quickly, and I wasn't ready to leave when our few days of sun, sand and surf were over. I wanted more time to walk in the warm backwash from the waves, lie on the sand, talk to my sister and make up for fifty years. But I had my flight booked and it was time to start thinking about going home. We took a slow drive back to Greensboro. We went via Red Springs, so that Jean and I could see the town together. She hadn't been back there for years and wanted to see it again. We stopped at the Dairy Ranch, a roadside café where they sell everything from fried catfish in brown paper bags, to fat slices of juicy watermelon. We ordered ice cream cones dipped in chocolate, because that was what she had from there when she was a little girl. It was hot so the ice cream was melting faster than we could eat it, and we laughed as the streams of melting ice cream ran down our wrists and dripped on our flip flops.

We got home late on Saturday evening, and I was leaving for England early on Monday morning. I only had one more day to spend with my sister. That Sunday was Fathers' Day. We ate breakfast early on the deck, in the cool shade. Jean told me how she had been feeling, sitting at the airport waiting for me to arrive. She was cross with herself. She had made that poster, "Welcome, Big Sister Perry" and had gotten everyone to sign it; she was going to take it to the airport so that she could hold it up and I would see it when I came out through those double doors. But she was nervous, a little panicky and in her panic, she had forgotten the poster, leaving it on the counter in the kitchen. When she realised, too far into the journey to the airport to go back for it, she had cried. Rob, ever the calming influence, had told her not to worry and suggested she call the boys and get them to put it up on the garage doors. They were not turning back to go and get it.

Sitting there at the airport, waiting, she had thought perhaps I wasn't coming because I had been such a long time coming through immigration. She had seen the plane land on time, and people had been steadily coming out into the Arrivals Hall, but still I hadn't come out through those doors. She had wondered if I had even been on the flight. Maybe I had chickened out. She told Rob, "The next person that comes through those doors, that's who we are taking home. I don't care if it's her or not!" Next through had been a large Filipino family with numerous children in tow. She and Rob had laughed, then.

She had started off sitting close to the double doors from where I would eventually be emerging. The seats were uncomfortable hard plastic, and she was fidgety. As time passed and I still hadn't appeared, she had found herself gradually moving down the row of seats towards the Exit. "That's me," she said, "Anything uncomfortable and I have to run away." She had said to Rob, "I can't do this." Every time he had looked away from her, she had moved a little closer to the Exit. "What are you going to do?" he had finally said to her, "You can't just leave her here." And then I had appeared, dragging my heavy bag with its extendable handle behind me. She had jumped up then, from her seat over by the Exit door to the safe outside world and she had just come right over, her feet hardly touching the ground. She surprised herself by doing that. No second thought, no looking back. Neither of us had looked back since that moment.

We went to church together on that last Sunday

morning to celebrate Fathers' Day. It was perfect; two daughters of the same father who had never known the other existed. I wondered what Eugene would have made of it, had he been there to see it. I had been through some extraordinary times on the journey to find my roots, and I knew that Jean's faith had sustained her not only through this, but through times of unimaginable horror during her life. Yes, celebrating Fathers' Day together in church with my sister was fitting.

After church we went for pizza. Al fresco in the shade of a giant parasol in the cool courtyard of the pizzeria, it was nicer than being inside the air-conditioned restaurant. I wanted to grab this one last opportunity of comfortable outdoor dining, because days like that would be few and far between back in England.

Lunch over, we went shopping. I needed some things to take home, chocolate mostly, but grits and barbecue sauce, marshmallow fluff and Twizzlers for my daughters. Then we went back to the house and I packed for the trip home. I stood on the bathroom scales, laughing, holding my weighty bag and I was two pounds over the limit for checked luggage. I needed a carry-on bag. Jean found one in her closet, and I rearranged my luggage. There was still room for the chocolate, which was in the fridge and would be packed last minute so it wouldn't melt.

My flight was departing early in the morning and I tried unsuccessfully to get a little sleep before leaving for the airport. It wasn't a direct flight back to England. I had to catch a connector flight to JFK Airport in New York. I would pick up my flight to London there. I was too wired to sleep. I was up long before I needed to be, drinking coffee, sitting on the edge of the bed and looking at my bags propped against the wall. I went downstairs and found the chocolate in the fridge. I stuffed it into my suitcase and hoped it wouldn't get crushed. When it was time to leave, we put my bags in the van. Rob driving, Jean in the back seat behind me. Just like it had been in what seemed like an age ago, when they had picked me up from the airport, but this time we didn't talk much. It may have been because it was so early in the morning, but I think we were all lost in our own thoughts. I didn't know how to say goodbye.

My last view of Jean and Rob was as I went through the security checkpoint in the Airport Terminal. We had hugged and cried, before finally letting go. I turned to wave as I took off my shoes to go through the metal detector and I could see them standing together behind the barrier. They waved back, then they turned away to leave. In the emotion of the moment, I left my shoes behind on the conveyor belt and had to be called back for them. I hadn't realised and probably would have boarded the plane in my socks. As I retrieved my shoes, I looked for my sister and her husband again, but they were gone. "That's me," I heard her saying in my head, "Anything uncomfortable and I have to run away." Shoes on, I turned and walked to the departure lounge, feeling an overwhelming sadness and wondering when I would get to see her again.

15

The Final Puzzle Piece

And so to the part about the (almost) Christmas baby. Since that day at Barnardo's headquarters in February 2008, when I had been handed my adoption file by Sue, I had been intrigued by the mystery couple Mr. and Mrs. Thurston. I had first discovered them in a fleeting reference on the first page of my file, *"After seeking the advice of a Moral Welfare Worker, the mother moved into a caravan owned by a Mrs. Thurston, taking the half-brother with her."* And then a little further down the page, *"She entered hospital for her confinement, the half-brother staying in the care of her landlady."* So Mrs. Thurston had looked after my half-brother George while Edith was in the hospital. Confinement: such a strange word, shut away from the world whilst giving birth. It's a medical term still sometimes in use today, but for me it spoke of the secrecy and shame surrounding my birth. Confined to a hospital room, the illegitimate child – the Bastard Baby - enters the world.

But that Mrs. Thurston; she didn't judge. She had looked after my half-brother George until both Edith and I were discharged from hospital on 19th December and we returned to the caravan. That's well over a week and what's more, she didn't press Edith for any rent money or keep because she knew she didn't have any. I felt Mrs. Thurston was a special lady.

Reading on through my adoption file, I came to a Dr. Barnardo's Homes memorandum dated 6th January 1959. *"Early yesterday, Mrs. Thurston, lately the mother's landlady, who has retained care of the Candidate* (me) *pending admission, telephoned and I later called on her and also on the Applicant.* (This was the Moral Welfare Worker).

"Mrs. Thurston explained that while the mother remained with her, she had received only the bare expenses of keeping the child. The mother had then returned to her own home, leaving Mrs. Thurston to care for the infant without payment.....

"The Applicant told me she realised how kind Mr. and Mrs. Thurston had been to the mother over so long a period – they had not known her at all until she had arrived to lodge in their caravan. They were most generous folk; but they could not be expected to bear the cost of temporarily maintaining the Candidate. Miss Tyler desired to make application, therefore, for a temporary grant to cover the cost. Mrs. Thurston had mentioned £2 per week towards which the mother should be contributing 8 shillings per week Family Allowance. Miss Tyler knew that the mother would be in some financial difficulties for a little while, until she could return to work and establish herself in her new home.

"Would it be possible to make the suggested temporary grant? Another aspect is that Miss Tyler understands that Mrs. Thurston would be prepared to become a local foster-mother and she does not wish a likely such helper to be upset at this stage...."

The contents of this memo were what had me reaching for the tissue box in the Making Connections office that day. Who were these people? They had taken my birth mother and my half-brother in, not knowing them – but more importantly not judging Edith for her circumstances. They didn't take rent for the caravan from her because they knew she was in financial hardship. They looked after George while Edith was in hospital, and then Edith left me, just a newborn baby, with them when she went back to Newbury.

They looked after me, and what is more they kept me until there was a space for me at St. Christopher's in late January 1959.

Reading on, it became apparent that Mrs. Thurston had herself actually taken me down to Kings Cross Station in London on the train from Beccles in Suffolk and handed me to the Barnardo's Travelling Matron for the final leg of my journey to St. Christopher's in Tunbridge Wells. This had not been straightforward either; the journey had to be delayed more than once because of snowstorms, and the Thurstons continued to keep me until the handover could be arranged.

I was bowled over by their kindness and generosity and I resolved, there and then, to one day find them and thank them for what they had done. They had to be very special people. Before that day I had no idea they even existed, and here they were, complete strangers, a hugely important part of my life story. I had always had the sense of being watched over, cared about and kept safe from harm right from the day I was born, and this confirmed it.

And so while I was busy seeking out my birth families, I was also looking for the Thurstons. Their address was on my birth certificate; The Log Cabin, Haddiscoe, Norfolk but that address no longer existed. At some time during the ensuing fifty years The Log Cabin had been demolished, re-named, or replaced. And there were no recent records of any Thurstons living in Haddiscoe. Census records yielded a number of people living together at Marsh Junction, Haddiscoe including some who were named Thurston. They were railway workers, but not in recent times. It did make sense though. I knew there had been old railway carriages on the land; my half-brother George had remembered playing in them, so perhaps Mr. Thurston had been a railway worker. Checking on Google Earth, I found a disused railway line running to the east of the village. It was had been part of the

London to Great Yarmouth line, which was closed in 1959 shortly after I was born. I checked the old phone directories and discovered that there were Thurstons listed at The Log Cabin until 1962, and then after that there was no trace of them. I wondered if they had been an elderly couple and had passed away. Perhaps I was to be years too late, but I really wanted to find them, and if they had children of their own I wanted to tell them how much I appreciated what their parents had done.

Eventually, with all my leads exhausted, there was nothing for it but to take myself off to Haddiscoe and see if I could find any trace of them, or the place that had been my home for the first few weeks of my life. It was a last-ditch effort, and I had to admit it felt like a bit of a long shot. It had been more than fifty years; that's half a century. I did some research and found that there were two pubs in the village. Pubs are always a good bet for locals with long memories, chatting over a pint of ale. One of the pubs advertised bed and breakfast rooms available. That would be perfect. I could stay at the pub and spend my evenings picking the brains of the customers. I telephoned the listed number, but there was no answer. I tried again a little later but there was still no answer. So instead, I called another local bed and breakfast establishment that I had found, and a very polite lady on the other end of the telephone informed me that they were no longer offering rooms. I mentioned the pub. "I wouldn't recommend it," she said. "I'll have a look at our local newsletter and see if I can find something else for you." How kind, I thought. These Haddiscoe people seemed like a friendly lot.

The nice lady gave me the telephone number of a bed and breakfast in a nearby village. She described it and it sounded lovely. "There are none in Haddiscoe now," she said, "I do hope you enjoy your visit." I telephoned and booked a room at the place she had recommended and resigned myself to driving into Haddiscoe to visit the local pubs.

And that is how, one evening in May 2011, I found myself sitting at the bar in the Crown Public House in Haddiscoe, Norfolk. My hopes of gleaning information from local people were dashed. There wasn't a single older local anywhere in sight, in fact there wasn't anyone who had even been born before 1960 in that pub, except for me. The bar was full of boisterous, rowdy, pool-playing teenagers and there was a huge flat screen television mounted on the wall with a football game playing. And loud music playing. The natives certainly looked friendly enough, but their memories would be far too short. I was thankful that I hadn't been able to book a room at the pub. The polite lady had said she wouldn't recommend it and I could see why. I would not have gotten much sleep.

The menu was typical British pub food. There was a blackboard on the wall listing everything that was available, and almost everything came with chips and peas, or just for something a little bit different, chips and baked beans. I went to the bar to order ham, egg, chips and peas at the bar and was promptly informed by the young blonde barmaid that they had run out of ham. I wondered how that could be possible in Norfolk – this was pork country and I had passed a massive pig farm on the way into the village. There were hogs everywhere in Norfolk, it seemed, except in the Crown. "We can do you a jumbo sausage, chips and beans," she suggested. Wondering what the sausage was made from and hoping it was pork, I nodded, paid for my food and thanked her. I went back to my dark red vinyl covered seat at the table in front of the television to watch the rest of the football game.

Eating my sausage, which was sadly less pork than cereal

and filler, I realised why the music was so loud. It was to cover the awful sounds made by the electric bug zapper situated directly underneath television. Attracted by the bright light, every time an unsuspecting insect flew into the thing there was a loud buzz as it was fried on the electrified grid within. Smoke and all. It was enough to put one off one's dinner. Giving up on the idea of chatting to the locals, I decided it was time to leave and drive back to my lodgings.

My very pleasant lodgings consisted of a room with adjoining bath in a wonderful, huge, quaint and slightly tatty old country house. It doubled as the home of the local vicar and his wife. Her name was interestingly, Buff and she was the font of all local knowledge. She also knew Peggy, the retired village post-mistress. Buff felt there was a good chance that Peggy would remember the Thurstons as she apparently knew everything about anybody who had ever lived within a thirty-mile radius of the village. Buff said she would check with Peggy in the morning.

I retired to my room, watched by Algernon the old family dog as I climbed the huge mahogany-railed staircase. Algae, or perhaps the correct spelling is Algie, as they called him, managed to thump his tail against the carpet a couple of times but mostly couldn't be bothered to get up. Just his eyes moved, following me up the stairs, like one of those old portraits hanging on the walls in stately homes.

Tired from my long drive up from Devon that day, I slept like a log in the massive carved mahogany four poster bed in my room. The next morning, after an enormous breakfast alone in the massive formal dining room at the head of what looked like a medieval banquet table, I was informed by Buff that she hadn't yet been able to contact Peggy. It was apparently Pension Collection Day, and Peggy would be going into Great Yarmouth on the bus. Ah well. I decided I would drive into Haddiscoe and see what I could find.

I had noticed a rather beautiful church in the village the previous day and thought I would start my search there. Churchyards and church records could provide a wealth of useful information. I had felt drawn to the church for some reason. I have always loved old English churches; as a child I remember being able to go into the church in the village where I grew up and sit in the cool stillness on a hot summer day. Nowadays churches are usually kept locked because of vandalism and theft. I have always thought that was rather sad, as an open church door somehow represents safety and shelter if there is nowhere else to go.

The church at Haddiscoe is over a thousand years old. It has a round tower made entirely from pebbles, which I thought was rather lovely. I drove down the bumpy lane to the car park. It wasn't too hard to find a parking space. There was only one other vehicle, a work van of some kind with a bored-looking man sitting in the driver's seat with one foot hanging out of the door. The church grounds had a slightly unkempt look, with weeds growing between the headstones and rabbit holes all over the place, even tunnelling under some of the monuments. I walked around the older part of the graveyard, looking for the name Thurston on the headstones. Lots of Buckinghams and Grimmers, but not a Thurston in sight, which I found slightly odd because Thurston is a relatively common name in Norfolk, if not in Haddiscoe itself. I wondered why I had felt so strongly drawn to the place, sure that there was something about this church that I was meant to discover.

I walked to the side of the church and stood in the porch, looking at the heavy ornately decorated ancient wooden door. Above the door was a carving in the stone. It looked like God, sitting on his throne in Heaven, holding the world in his upraised hands. I thought I would try the latch on the door, more than half-expecting it to be locked. There was a loud "thlunk" as the latch lifted, and I pushed the heavy door open and walked inside. It was cool in there. The walls of the nave were white – clean and simple, plain dark wooden pews and a beautiful dark wood roof which looked like the inside of an upturned boat. There was a table to the rear of the pews with some little prayer cards and leaflets on it. "It is our policy to keep the church unlocked, please respect it", I was informed by a small handwritten card. There was a guestbook which I signed. I wrote a short note that I was looking for some very special people who I felt sure were connected with the church. I walked down towards the altar, looking at the beautiful stained-glass window up behind it, and said a silent prayer that my day would be fruitful.

Back to the car. The man was still there in his van; he hadn't moved, and his leg was still hanging out of the door. I got into my car and drove off towards the main part of the village, not really knowing where to begin. I thought I might drive to where the disused railway cut through close to the village and look for old wooden buildings and abandoned railway carriages. It did seem rather random and hopeless, but I had to begin somewhere. I turned into a tiny lane almost directly opposite the Crown pub. Low Road. It seemed to run in the approximate direction of the old railway line. There were lots of old shacks and a lot of undergrowth, or rather overgrowth. Funny – it reminded me of the day out at Back Swamp with my aunts Martha and Jolene.

As I drove slowly along the lane, I noticed on my left a fenced-in piece of land with a couple of old caravans sitting on it. The land had been cleared of trees and undergrowth, but the caravans looked derelict. There was an old man, or maybe a woman – I couldn't be sure from the distance, but in any case, this person was wearing shorts and pushing a wheelbarrow across the rear of the property towards a small bonfire. I made a mental note to stop there later, if the person was still around, after I had finished my tour around the lanes of Haddiscoe.

I drove out to the nearby Waveney River Centre on the Norfolk Broads, had a walk around the marina and admired the boats. Some of them were what are termed "live-aboards", with people living on board year-round. Those boats had colourful flower gardens in pots and planters all over their decks. It was nice, and I was having a lovely time in the warm sunshine, but I wasn't getting anywhere with my search, so I drove back to the village. The blonde barmaid from the Crown was outside on the pub patio, setting up parasols over the tables. I parked in the pub car park – a little cheeky of me, but then I could always get a drink there after my walkabout. I crossed the main road and walked down Low Road to see if I could find the one other person I had seen that day apart from the barmaid.

He or she was still there, down at the back of the plot of land, tending to the bonfire. There was a little old wooden shack down there, and I wondered if the person lived there. I opened the small metal gate at the front of the property and walked down the field towards the person and the bonfire. As I got closer, the person turned towards me and I saw it was a woman; tanned and muscular and weathered, but most of all, old. She was the right age to remember the Thurstons. I felt a little foolish, but I was compelled to ask her anyway. I smiled at her as I approached, and she smiled back. One of those friendly Haddiscoe people, I realised with some relief. She wasn't going to make a rush for the front porch of the shack and grab a shotgun, like Granny Clampett from the Beverly Hillbillies would have done. Strange, the things that go through your mind.

"I know this sounds silly", I began, "But do you know

of a place called The Log Cabin in the village?" She thought for a few seconds and then said, "I think it was up near the church. It's not there now." Taking the plunge, I asked her if she knew of the Thurstons.

"Ah", she said, and her face lit up, "You mean Reggie and Eva. Evangeline, her name was. She died some years back. Reggie died a little while ago, too. They have a son and a daughter still living in Gorleston somewhere." I was completely amazed that she had known them. I told her a little bit of why I was trying to find them; that they had looked after me when I was a baby.

"You need to talk to Colin," she said, "Colin can help you more. They were good friends." She directed me to a bungalow on a tiny lane opposite the turning to the church. "I can't remember what the house number is, or what the road name is, but that's where it is." she said. I thanked her and went back to my car, scarcely believing my luck.

I found the bungalow – it had a nameplate on it, AT-LE-DO. An unusual house name, I thought it must be a play on words for "That'll do". It made me smile.. I walked up to the front door and knocked. A tiny woman opened the door. I said, "Hello, I'm looking for Colin." "Yes, this is where he lives," the little woman said, "He's my husband. But he's not here." I told her I was looking for where The Log Cabin used to be, and the people that used to live there, the Thurstons. "They used to live here," she said, "Reggie built this bungalow after they moved out of The Log Cabin. It was just down behind here."

The woman's name was Geena. Standing there on the doorstep, I told her a little bit about my story; how the Thurstons had cared for me before I was adopted and that I wanted to thank them, but I knew they had both passed away. "Come in," Geena said, "I'm good friends with their daughter, Margaret. I can put you in touch with her. She lives in Gorleston."

I went into the neat and tidy bungalow and Geena made us a cup of tea. She brought through a plate of biscuits, and we sat together in the living room which overlooked the little valley behind the bungalow. She pointed out of the large picture window. "That's where The Log Cabin was," she said, "Where that new bungalow is now. The Log Cabin was two old railway carriages stuck together; that's where they lived. It was sold off, and the railway carriages were taken away before the bungalow was built."

I asked if I could have Margaret's address so that I could contact her. "I'll phone her," Geena said, and she promptly picked up the phone and dialled Margaret's number. Margaret answered. "It's Geena," said my new friend, "I've got a lady here says your mum and dad looked after her at The Log Cabin before she was adopted. Best I just hand you over." And she gave me the phone. I said a tentative, "Hello?" It all seemed rather amazing suddenly. Margaret responded with an equally tentative, "Hello?", so I said, "Hello Margaret, my name is Perry…" and I heard her sharp intake of breath at the other end of the phone. She started crying. For some reason, so did I. "You kept the name," she said. "You were the first….. we always wondered what had happened to you. We loved you so much, Mum loved you. We all did."

We talked. She remembered how it had been just before Christmas, and her mum had said, "What are we to do, Reggie? The baby has nowhere to go. Christmas is all about a baby, isn't it? And this is a baby, isn't it? We'll keep her." And that is how the decision was made. They had nothing ready for me, so I slept in a drawer because there was no cot. They had very little of anything, they lived in two old railway carriages with their own children, yet they had taken no money from my mother. Margaret told me she used to hold me, and feed me, and bathe me. She said, "Mum fostered lots of babies after you. I used to go with her down to London on the train and she would hand them over at Kings Cross station. Every time she did it, she broke her heart and she would sit on a bench at the station and cry. Then we'd go shopping to cheer us both up."

I asked her if I could come and see her that evening. "'Course you can," She said. "I've got a suitcase full of photographs." Photographs, the icing on the cake! I was so excited. We arranged a time, I got directions and we said goodbye until later. "Now," said Geena, "Drink your tea and I'll phone Peter at the bungalow down there. Peter and his wife live there now. You can go and see where The Log Cabin used to be."

16

Always Loved

Peter at the bungalow was slightly bemused at first, I think. We sat on his shady patio drinking tea and I told him my story. Bemusement turned to fascination. He told me that he and his wife had only lived in the bungalow for four years, having retired to Norfolk from London, and they were really enjoying the slower pace of life. Before they had bought the place, it had been a little run down and not too much remained now of how it used to be. They had renovated the inside of the bungalow and had beautifully landscaped the terraced gardens which ran up the side of the little valley. "It's strange," he said, "We always had the feeling that there was something special about this place, as if it had a story."

He had shown me around the bungalow. The property was beautiful inside and out, a far cry from those two old railway carriages, I am sure. He told me a story. "We were told that the chap who bought this land from the Thurstons tried for a long time to get planning permission to build a proper house. The railway carriages were still here then, but the council kept refusing his application because there was technically already a dwelling on the property. So he set fire to the carriages and burned them to the ground, then he went back to the council and asked them if they were satisfied. He got his planning permission then, and that's how this place came to be built." He added, "I'm not sure if any of that's true, but that's the rumour we heard." I really hoped that it wasn't. I had always harboured romantic notions about The Log Cabin, and although I now know that was a far cry from the truth, I had a fondness in my heart for the place, and it was the address on my birth certificate. It would have been a sad end indeed.

Peter left me to wander around the gardens. I thought I could still see where the caravan had stood, and I walked along the little path to what was now a neat vegetable patch. The footings for the caravan were still there. I turned around and looked back towards the bungalow. There, framed by a beautiful rose arch was a view of the pebble tower of the church across the road. It was a beautiful and it took my breath away. This would have been what Edith would have seen every morning as she stepped outside the caravan; that wonderful old church tower that I had been so drawn to. There can't have been a better view of it from anywhere else in the village.

There were still lots of old railway sleepers in the garden, tiering and terracing the colourful flower beds on their way up the side of the steep little valley. I wondered if these were survivors from The Log Cabin; Geena had told me Reggie and Eva had added a small kitchen extension onto their railway carriages and I felt sure they must have used the old sleepers to do this. Perhaps that was why they had called it The Log Cabin. What a privilege to have this small insight into the way they had lived. I never dreamed I would have the opportunity to see and experience this, and I was very grateful to Peter for opening up his home to me that afternoon.

We had more tea and biscuits on the patio, and then I said my goodbyes. I drove back to my lodgings and told an excited Buff about my day. She hadn't been able to make contact with Postmistress Peggy, but I said if she did, I would still love to meet her. "She'll probably bring her latest boyfriend," said Buff, "He's eighty-seven, this boyfriend. She gets a new one every time one passes away. This must be number six at least."

Half an hour later I was on my way to Gorleston to meet Margaret. I was early but I just wanted to get there. I thought I would get my bearings and then maybe grab some fish and chips to eat on the Promenade at the seafront before I went to her house, just to soak in a bit of the seaside atmosphere of Gorleston and gather my thoughts.

I found my fish and chips supper and went for a walk on the beach. It was still gloriously sunny in the early evening. I took off my shoes and the sand felt warm underfoot. The sandy beach stretched for miles ahead of me, and apart from one or two distant dog walkers and some joggers up above on the Promenade I had the place all to myself. Miles of golden sand stretched ahead of me, and I strolled slowly along, thinking about the incredible few hours that had just passed. I had set out for Norfolk hoping for the impossible – what were the chances, really, of me finding this family who had taken me in? I had put on a brave face with my own family and told them I felt I had to give finding them this one last-ditch attempt. I think they thought I had lost my mind. I would never have felt I had done everything I possibly could if I hadn't come. But the truth is that I didn't hold out much hope. At worst, I reasoned, it would be a much-needed short break in a beautiful part of the country that I hadn't spent enough time exploring in the past. I couldn't believe how it had all come together so perfectly, and now I was going to meet the daughter of those wonderful people who had cared for me as a newborn baby.

I walked back to my car and made the short drive to Margaret's house. I found the street easily and drove along the quiet dead-end road looking for the right house number. The houses all looked very similar to each other; traditional 19th century terraced townhouses, very practical in design and really only to be told apart by the different coloured front doors and the occasional hanging basket. There were no driveways here, it was street parking only. The original occupants of these row houses had no need of a garage or parking space because they had no cars. I found Margaret's house and a convenient parking space a little further down the road. I walked back to her house, opened the front gate and walked up to the door, which opened before I could knock. There stood a woman I hadn't seen for fifty-two years. She had been nine years old when her mum and dad had fostered me; just a little girl. Two small dogs were running around our feet. We hugged like old friends and she invited me in. I noticed the battered suitcase propped up against the stairs in the hallway. "Photographs," she said, catching my gaze, "I've been going through that all afternoon, ever since I spoke to you. I've got some for you."

We went into the cosy living room with the dogs bouncing around us, excited. A tiny Yorkshire Terrier puppy, Rolfie; and a very handsome and rather long-suffering Tibetan Spaniel called Tyson. Poor Tyson was getting the brunt of Rolfie's boisterous attentions and was probably more than happy to have me there as a distraction. After a few minutes he plopped himself down and watched me contentedly from across the room as Rolfie climbed, bounced, yipped and did everything he could think of, to get my full attention. I laughed. Margaret's husband made us a cup of tea. Margaret said,

"I can't believe you are here. I was only talking about you last week." I found this incredulous. She explained, "My friend at work is adopted. She has some problems. I told her all about you, how Mum and Dad took you in." I began to realise that in some way, although my time with the Thurstons was only measured in weeks, that time had made a tremendous impact on all our lives.

Margaret talked me through it. "You were the first," she said. "If it hadn't been for you, Mum would never have fostered all those babies. She became a local foster parent for Barnardo's. I don't remember all the babies; some of them came with nothing. There were loads of them over the years. We never forgot you, though."

Margaret's daughter Cassie arrived. "I'm so happy to finally meet you after hearing about you for all these years," she said. A beautiful girl in her twenties, so striking. She sat down opposite me. I felt like I had come home. Margaret said, "I feel like I've always known you; after all, we were sisters for a short while." And yes, it really did feel like that.

I was very anxious to see the photos. They were in a pile on the coffee table in front of me. I wanted to know what Reggie and Eva looked like. And I was hoping there would be photographs of me, in the early weeks of my life. My mum and dad had pictures, yes. But the earliest of these were of me as an older baby when they used to visit me every week at St. Christopher's in Tunbridge Wells, before they were finally able to foster me and eventually adopt me. I was at least several months old in those photographs. Margaret handed me the first picture. It was Eva sitting in a comfortable armchair, holding a tiny scrap of a baby. The little naked thing was looking up at her face. The baby's left foot was turned in at an odd angle. It was me as a newborn. Eva, with dark hair and dark rimmed glasses, smiling.

"This is Mum and Dad," said Margaret, handing me the next black and white print. A handsome couple in their thirties, standing close together, she is smiling, he is looking a little serious. Tall and slim. They looked to be in a kitchen. "That was the kitchen in The Log Cabin," said Margaret.

Another photograph of Eva, sitting laughing in the comfy chair. "That was where Mum used to feed the babies, in that chair," explained Margaret, "If you look at the right of the picture, that door is one of the original doors in the railway carriage," she said.

And then she handed me a photograph of a girl aged about nine or ten, all dark fringe flopping over her eyes, holding a small baby. "That's me," Margaret said, "Holding you." I was so moved I couldn't speak. Tears came. I reached for the handy box of tissues. Again, I thought how incredible this all was, not only had I found them, but they had photographs which had survived all these years. And here I was with this woman, fifty-two years on, who had held me as a tiny newborn baby and had the photo to prove it.

"I remember your brother George," she said. "He went to school with us. Tell him I'm sorry I was so mean to him when you speak to him." She laughed. "We were just kids," she said. Then she told me of a memory she had of George. "He saw you, you know. I had to tell him, 'Don't blow on the baby's face, you'll scare her.' He never knew you were his sister." So George had actually seen me and had even interacted with me. I wondered if he would remember any of this if I told him. He had been a little vague when I had spoken to him, remembering the caravan and the railway carriages, and seeing a baby but little else. But then that comment he had made about ladies getting fat when they had babies. I wondered if, memory jogged a little, George would recall anything more.

Out came more photographs. The tiny caravan. "That was the first one," said Margaret. "But it had no heating, and it was so small for her and George. It was getting into winter," she said, "They were with us for quite a few months. Dad had a bigger caravan moved on for her. One with some heat." And she produced another photograph of a caravan, with a man sitting on the steps, smiling. A much bigger and more modern-looking caravan altogether. "That was my granddad," Margaret explained. So they had not only taken Edith and George in and looked after them for free, they had even found a bigger and more suitable caravan for them. What incredible people. They never judged her, and they gave her a real chance to see the absolute best in people at a very difficult time in her life. These were not affluent people giving out of their wealth. They had little themselves, and yet still they gave. Humbling. I said to Margaret, "You know, I have always felt like I was looked after. I always felt loved, despite being given up. Now I think I know why."

We talked about Edith. I wanted to know what Margaret remembered of her. Margaret didn't recall very much. She was a small child and remembered far more of George than she did of his mother. She knew that her mother and Edith had become friends and had stayed in touch for quite a few years after my adoption. They used to write to each other and kept in touch regularly until Edith had gotten married and moved to America. "She sent us some American chewing gum," recalled Margaret. There was another photograph of Edith, standing in a garden with a huge pampas grass in the background; Edith, George and an older man. At the time I thought perhaps he may have been Edith's older brother. Later I discovered that the man was Edith's father, which made him my maternal grandfather. There was a note written on the back of that photograph in Edith's distinctive hand. "Hasn't George grown?" So she hadn't just run off and abandoned me, then. "No," said Margaret, "She was around quite often after you were born. She bought you an outfit. I remember." She must have made trips back up to Norfolk to see me, then.

Of course, this did not add up with Sandra's description of her mother. I was finding it very hard to reconcile the cruel, hard and unfeeling woman described to me by Sandra with this woman who had stayed in touch with Margaret's mother, had ensured I had somewhere safe to be left, and had even cared enough to buy me something nice to wear. I believe, though, that the ensuing years must have taken their toll on Edith and the memories may have been too much for her to bear. A violent marriage, the loss of her infant son Arthur, and then having a daughter she had to give up and walk away from. In my heart I now believe that she ran away and tried to put it all behind her; cutting herself off from anything that could remind her of these tragic events. And she did it, but at what cost? I felt terribly sad for her and wished again I had had the chance to meet her and speak with her.

We talked lots about Margaret's parents, the wonderful Eva and Reggie. They had been well known and well loved in the village of Haddiscoe before moving into Gorleston more than thirty years before. Margaret handed me another photograph, the first colour photo I had seen from the suitcase, of a laughing middle-aged Reggie and Eva relaxing on a beach towel, the sun shining, they looked so carefree. And then she gave me a newspaper cutting; a write-up from their 50th Wedding Anniversary. They were of course much older then; Eva was very thin. Margaret said, "That wasn't too long before she died." Eva had passed away some years before from cancer. Reggie had moved in next door to Margaret and her husband. He had only died the previous year, and I had just missed meeting him. "I wish you could have," said Cassie, "He was a wonderful man; he had a great sense of humour." "Mum would have been so proud of you," added Margaret, "She used to say whenever there was anyone on TV with the name 'Perry', 'I wonder if that's her? She's about the right age.' And I would say, 'Don't be silly, Mum. They won't have kept the name.' But you did." I told her how my mum and dad had loved the name and decided to keep it, and I'm so glad they did. I wished I could have found out why Edith had given me that name; it must have meant something to her, but I doubt now that I will ever know. That was one secret that died with Edith, and if she remembered, she never said so when Sandra finally asked her about me.

I had a wonderful evening with Margaret and Cassie, and the two crazy little dogs. I didn't want to leave. Margaret had accepted me into her home like I was family, just as her own parents had done for my birth mother so many years before. Margaret and Cassie feel like family to me. Margaret answered so many questions that I've wanted answers to for my whole life in that one short evening together, and I hope to always stay in touch with her. She is yet another sister for me.

17

Loose Ends

After I returned to England from my epic American trip, my sister Jean and I embarked on a quest to retrieve Eugene's military records. We were hoping to shed some light on the reason he was sent back to America in 1958. Jean remembers him writing a letter to appeal some form of dishonourable marker on his military record. She believes he was sent back to America after beating up a woman. That is her recollection. This made me wonder if it were Edith. Sadly, our application has so far come to nothing. The records of his military service appear to have been lost. In 1973 there was a fire at the National Personnel Records Center in St. Louis, Missouri. Millions of service history files for servicemen discharged between 1912 and 1964 were permanently lost, including, it would seem, Eugene's. It is as if he were never even in the Air Force and never in Britain. Yet we know that he was, and there are photographs of him proudly wearing his uniform as a young man. And then there is that photograph of him, standing outside a building at the Newbury air base, hands in pockets, carefree and smiling widely at the camera, with the blue "x" above his head.

I went to the air base, RAF Greenham Common in Berkshire. It's not very far from where Sandra and Henry still live. It is decommissioned now but many of the original buildings are still there. The base has quite a history. It was built in 1942 during the Second World War and had the longest military runway in Europe, specially designed to take heavy bombers. The American Ninth Air Force took the base over in 1943 and stayed for the duration of the War. The base was then handed back to the Royal Air Force and mothballed for five years, but with the advent and escalation of the Cold War the United States Air Force came back to Greenham Common and stayed in one form or another until 1992, when the base was finally deactivated.

There had been a nuclear incident there in February of 1958 and I'm presuming that Eugene was there when that happened. When he was based there, Greenham Common was a Strategic Air Command heavy bomber base, with fully fuelled and nuclear-armed B-47 Stratojet bombers on standby, ready to take off at a moment's notice to drop their lethal payload on the Soviet Union in the event of war. I believe Eugene was part of the base support group responsible for non-flying activities, maintenance and logistics. In any case, he didn't fly. He may have had a lucky escape that February. A B-47 bomber flying over the airfield had accidentally jettisoned a wing-tip fuel tank loaded with aviation fuel. It hit the ground close behind another bomber which was carrying an armed nuclear bomb and was waiting for clearance to take off. The fuel tank exploded when it hit the ground and engulfed the waiting plane, and the nuclear bomb. The conventional explosive in the warhead went off, scattering uranium and plutonium particles over a wide area, and the bomb burned, contaminating an area of several square miles around the base. The resulting fire burned for five days and several service personnel on the ground were killed.

Later, beginning in the early 1980's, the airfield gained notoriety as one of the designated bases for ground launched

American nuclear cruise missiles. Reinforced bunkers for the missiles were built and are still in existence today. The entire area was swamped for years with peace protesters. These became popularly known as the Greenham Common Peace Women, and they stayed encamped around the base until after the missiles were finally removed between 1989 and 1991. The Defence Ministry then sold off the majority of the site in 1992 to private enterprise.

In July 2011, with the Americans, the Peace Women and the cruise missiles long gone, the base still has a certain military ambience. I was surprised to find that many of the original buildings are still there and looking not that much changed. The control tower, the base post office, the chapel, even the ballroom, all still there. Many of the old barracks and offices are still there too, occupied now by small and eclectic businesses – a dance school, a gym, a coffee shop. But the streets still have American style names like Main Street, Fifth Avenue, Third Street. It's easy to imagine oneself transported back to the 1950's; to imagine the personnel all still there, the noise of the B-47 bombers winding up for take-off on the runway in the background, men in uniform walking on the sidewalks going about their business, Edith working away at her typewriter in her office in one of those buildings, with her Dr. Barnardo's collection box on her desk. The lie of the land really hasn't changed that much in over fifty years.

I had gone looking for the building in the photograph. I had thought how amazing it would be to have a photograph of me, standing in that exact spot where Eugene had stood all those years ago, hands in pockets and looking like he had not a care in the world. It was raining on the day I was there. Typical English summertime weather. A July deluge, in fact. I got out of the car, leaving the engine running and windscreen wipers on high speed, and took off running across the grass to get the best shot of each potential building. I realised that I was being observed with some hilarity by the dry people inside the buildings, sitting at their desks, having a coffee and wondering what on earth the mad middle-aged woman in shorts and tee shirt was doing out there in the pouring rain. I can't honestly say I found the exact spot, but I did find a building that could have been the right one, with the old aluminium windows now painted black, and the downspout and guttering replaced with something a little more modern and plastic than the cast iron downspout in the background of the photograph. Was it the right place? I don't know. It's called the Body Conditioning Centre now. But it was a strange experience to stand there in the pouring rain and think that Eugene as a young man may have stood in that same spot with the sun shining more than fifty years before.

On the long drive back to Devon that day, it occurred to me again that this is not just my story. If I had not started the search, setting the wheels in motion, not only would my own life have been less than fulfilled today, but the lives of the people I have found along the way would not have been changed in the ways that they have. And mostly, that has been for the better. My adopted sister has never had any desire to seek out her roots or trace her birth family. More than that, she cannot understand why I would have wanted to. She feels very strongly that seeking out her birth family would be a betrayal of our parents' love, although happily Mum had been enthralled by it all and actively involved in it from the day that I got my adoption file. My sister simply cannot understand this. "I don't want to know where I came from, I'm happy with what I've got, and why change that?" Beginning a search is not a decision to take lightly and there are always doubts and fears about what – and who - we may discover along the way. But if we don't, what about those other pieces of the puzzle that may never fall into place? Not just our pieces, but those belonging to the other players; people who were a part of our past lives and may have issues of their own waiting to be resolved. I know it's not for everyone, but in my case, despite the emotional rollercoaster that I sometimes wondered if I would ever get off, I'm so glad I went looking.

We live in such an egocentric and hedonistic culture; self-serving, self-seeking, self-entitled. The focus of our daily lives is the advancement of our personal gain. Did I start my search with that goal of being self-fulfilled subconsciously in my mind? Was I doing it for a feeling of self-justification perhaps? Certainly, I wanted to find out more about me and I accomplished that, but if my motivation was selfish at the beginning, I certainly got a rude awakening. As my American sister Jean said, "I don't know what questions you have that I can answer in a way that will put a smile on your face or uplift your spirits. I'm not sure you really want to know what it was like…" By that time of course, I already knew that Eugene was dead, and I already knew this was no fairy-tale. But it has made me think about my own motives and what I believe was an almost instinctive deep-rooted need to find out where I "fit" in this world. We all need to belong.

I have often wondered why the door to my past was so firmly closed when I went knocking years ago as a teenager. I can see now that the timing was all wrong; if not for me, then for my American sisters and my aunts. They would not have been ready to hear from me and the door would have been slammed shut, perhaps never to reopen. I believe the whole search journey would have ended prematurely. None of us would have found any meaningful reconciliation with our past lives. I am very much aware that there are greater forces in the Universe at work than we can understand, but for anything to happen we must first be brave and take that initial step.

EPILOGUE

There really is no ending to The (Almost) Christmas Baby, because my life story and the stories of the other people I have discovered along the way are still being written. There are those who haven't yet wanted to be a part of this story and maybe they never will. It's all still unfolding. I kept a journal every day when I began researching; documenting everything that happened as well as my thoughts and feelings in the moment. I did the same whenever I was traveling and when I met my biological families. Keeping that journal was the best thing I ever did, because every detail is written down, every feeling documented. It formed the basis for much of this book. When I started putting it all together as a project, there was a need to record what was happening emotionally to me because it was all so big, and there were times when it felt a little out of control. When I started writing, I felt like the story was bursting out of me like a river though the floodgates, and it would be a tragedy if no-one else knew about it. I didn't want anything to be lost. I wanted to document and share every detail with my own family and especially with my daughters, because my roots are their roots too.

It also occurred to me that I might be able to encourage other people to start or continue their own searches, so I also wanted to share this journey with those outside of my own personal circle. There were so many babies, and some older children too, adopted in the 50's and 60's when adoptions outside of the natural family peaked. Often before that time, larger families "absorbed" children – for example, if an older daughter had a baby, that child might be retained within the family but raised as a younger sibling of the natural mother and may never have known any differently. This was all of course before the advent of birth control and abortion, both of which curtailed the flow of babies being given up for adoption. There are a lot of us out there, now in our sixties and seventies, from those days. It has surprised me how many people I know personally who have only told me that they are adopted since they found out that I am, and that I have been writing my story. Although we have moved on considerably from the stigma of the past, adoption still seems to be something which people are reluctant to share. Why is that? Perhaps we are still struggling with the labels of the past when most babies who were given up for adoption were those of illegitimate birth, and therefore labelled as the product of a sinful relationship. The child was thought of as tainted by the sinful act of the people who created him or her. The term "bastard" is an interesting one. As an adjective, it means debased, irregular, inferior, of questionable origin, no longer in its pure or original form. As a noun it is a derogatory term meaning an unpleasant or despicable person. There is nothing positive to be gleaned from that word, and somehow even the redeeming act of placing that child into a different family unit did nothing to dispel the shame of the child's beginnings. Even today in more enlightened times, changes need to be made. For example, a child adopted into the peerage still cannot inherit a title. An adopted child should not be any less deserving than a natural one.

Now, with the available technology and a more open society, we have a unique opportunity to look back at our beginnings if we choose to. Many more recently adopted children have what is termed an "open adoption", where there is some degree of contact between the child, the adoptive parents and the natural mother or both birth parents. This can range from one simple phone call between the two families after the adoption placement is made, to ongoing visits throughout the child's life. It is 'not a one size fits all" situation. For some parents and adopted children, this is beneficial but for others it makes for complication and confusion. Decisions are driven not by the child, but by the adults in the child's life, and sometimes it all sadly ends up in the courts. As a great many adoptions do not now involve adoption agencies like Barnardo's but are privately arranged, many jurisdictions do have a requirement for the full names of birth parents to be provided to the adopted person when they reach the age of majority. This is a good thing for those children who do want to know more, as it alleviates the need to search for original names and birth certificates. This can still be difficult but in general the door to the past, once firmly closed when the adoption was finalised, has now been unbolted and even opened a crack with changes in legislation over recent years. Now, all we have to do is push the door, let it open and walk on through. Of course, we can never know ahead of time what we might discover, so the first step through the doorway is a big one, and not to be taken lightly. Some of us will look at the door and think perhaps it is best left locked, like my adopted sister. Or, as in my case, some of us will look at it for years and wonder what would happen if we dared to open it. Sue, my social worker from Barnardo's, gave me some sobering advice. She said that if I were to choose to follow through and seek out members of my birth family, that I owed it to the people I find to not turn my back on them and walk away. In other words, if you open the door, you don't get to slam it shut again if you don't like what you find. Having said all that, I believe that the fear of the unknown is generally greater than the unknown itself. Don't expect a fairy-tale because that's just not real life, but whatever and whomever you find, remember that they're a part of your story, good or bad. In my own experience, making the decision to open the door is the hardest part. Once it's open, the path is there to explore and we just have to be willing to walk wherever it takes us. Yes, we may stumble, trip and even fall, we may pause before moving forward and we may even get hurt along the way, but for me the journey has been worth it, every bump and bruise. If you are lucky, you may find healing, or perhaps others who are a part of your story may find some healing themselves. Sometimes we don't see that happening at the time, because healing is a process, but with time to reconcile what we find out about ourselves and others, it may come.

It is my fervent hope that my story will encourage and inspire. My wish is that they – the ones who want to know but have been fearful of pushing the door open – will be brave enough to follow their hearts and not be put off by fear of the unknown. It honestly cannot be any more of an emotional rollercoaster than my journey, and not only did I survive but I don't regret any of it for one second. For some, it will be enough just to know what happened when they were given up, perhaps to get the records of their adoptions, discover the circumstances and not follow up any further. For some, that's a first step but it needs to go deeper. I believe for many of us there's an inherent feeling of rejection that goes along with being adopted. This is something I struggled with over the years despite being raised in a loving family. What did I do, that made my mother give me up? Sometimes there is a need for reassurance that it wasn't our fault, and really how can it have been? It's not like we had any choice in the matter. It's always down to circumstances, and as in Edith's case, those were insurmountable at the time for her. Yes, sometimes it gets painful when we dig deep, but I have said more than once that, difficult as this has been at times, I have no regrets. I cannot fathom life not knowing all this, good and bad, and not finding all the people I have found who are a part of me, and a part of my story.

I waited until my dad had passed away before opening the door to my past. I am still not sure he would have been completely on board with it, but I had a feeling that Mum would, and I was right. I didn't tell her anything about it until I had my adoption file in my hands, and I took it over to her and sat her down to tell her all about it. Then I gave her the entire file and let her read it. She was like a child herself, reading the letters that Dad had written to Barnardo's when they first applied to adopt, reading the reports of the home visits they had literally endured, when a Moral Welfare Worker would drop by unannounced to see how I was doing in their care. There were things she had forgotten about, and her face lit up more than once as she was reminded of them. She said she thought that Dad would have been pleased, and that meant a lot to me. Mum kept the file for a few weeks to read it all through, and again the timing for all this was perfect. Had I waited any longer she may never have been able to do that, because she suddenly lost her sight a few months later.

One of the hardest things for me to come to terms with has been not being able to see Edith before she died. I really would have given anything to be able to sit with her for a while and tell her that I never blamed her for what she had to do. There are questions I wanted to ask her. For example, why did she name me Perry? Was I named after a person, a place, something or someone important to her? It seems to me that it was a very deliberate choice she made. This has followed me throughout my life because my unusual name has always been a talking point. I cannot count the times I have silently thanked my mum and dad for choosing to keep the name. It was brave of them not to want to completely expunge my past and give me an entirely new identity. Most often with adoptions, especially babies, the new parents want to choose the name for their child and so the original birth name is changed. Like me, I feel my name is a little "different", and I would have loved to have known where it came from. I will have to settle for the fact that it will now remain forever a mystery. I suppose that even if I had got to meet Edith at the age of 89, she may not have remembered any of it, but I would love to have had the chance to ask.

There is a big part of me that believes Edith married and left England for America to run away from what had happened. Sandra has told me that Edith wanted nothing to do with her own granddaughter, English Jean, when she was a little girl. Jean had been born in July, just a few months before me. In Sandra's words, Edith hated little girls and she didn't even want to see her. Little wonder really, when she had given up a baby girl of her own just a few short months after Jean was born. Sandra's perception was that Edith liked boys better. She told me that Edith was never so cruel to George as she had been to her. Edith had also told George that she only married again to get her ticket out of England, and she had never loved her new husband, Roy. She told Sandra she only married him for his chequebook and the stability he could offer. After she left, Edith only came back to England once, for the funeral of a family member (I don't know who that was, but perhaps her father), and she never set foot on English soil again. She cut all ties with everybody she knew and even didn't speak to Sandra for a number of years.

Sandra has said that Edith was always a cruel, hard and calculating woman. I know Sandra still loved her mother deeply despite everything, but I do wonder whether that is who Edith became after being dealt such a rough hand in life. Our experiences do shape and change us. Our circumstances help to make us who we are. We develop behaviours and coping strategies especially after we have suffered trauma or been deeply hurt. The woman who fled from her abusive husband, taking her children with her and starting a new life as a single mother speaks of single-minded determination and resolve. Not hardness or cruelty, but strength and courageousness. But it all went wrong. Sandra, just a teenager, got pregnant and was married off, a shotgun wedding if you like, and then Edith ironically found herself in the same position just a few months later but there was to be no shotgun wedding for her. No wonder she hid the pregnancy and gave me up. She had already lost one child, Arthur, between Sandra and George, and now she had to lose another one. I cannot even imagine the strength she would have needed to get through all that, without any family support or professional counselling.

In recent years there has been a surge of interest in ancestry, roots and family connections; everything from television shows about celebrities tracing their family histories to mothers and babies separated at birth being reunited. Since I have been speaking openly about my story, I have discovered people in my own circle who gave up babies – people who have come to me and told me their own stories of having to part with a child. They found themselves in difficult circumstances or bowing to family pressure to give their baby up. It is not that uncommon a situation, but I have been struck by the commonality of the message from those women who have given up a baby for one reason or another. They all want to know the answer to the same set of questions. What happened to my child? Is he or she alright? Does he or she have a good life? Does my child blame me? Every single birthday that comes and goes for that child, the mother would think about him or her, and wonder. I cannot ever really know whether Edith wondered about these things; it is possible that she did not, but the chances are that she did. I have seen the carefully worded handwritten notes from her in my adoption file, enquiring about my progress and asking for a Barnardo's collection box to place in her office. I've met someone, Margaret, who knew her after I was given up, who tells me she bought me a special outfit to wear before she went back to her job at the air base. I don't think she ever forgot about me, although she may have locked me away somewhere in the back of her mind as a coping strategy and then one day forgot where she had put the key.

I would have loved to have told Edith in person that I never blamed her, and I hope that she didn't blame herself, although I suspect she probably did. And I suspect that my birth radically changed the direction of her life and affected everyone else around her, including Sandra and George. Would I be wrong to speculate that she may have covered up her pain with a hard uncaring exterior? Perhaps I am oversimplifying things.

Sandra says she believes Edith buried the painful memories so deeply that she truly couldn't remember them, and I do believe Sandra was very fearful of what may transpire if certain memories was triggered by my reappearance. Sandra believes if there was any recollection in our mother's mind of the circumstances surrounding my birth, it was best she died believing she had kept her secret buried and had never been found out. I hope it's true that by then she really didn't remember, because the alternative is too painful to think about.

I've been back and revisited my relationship with Sandra. We didn't really get off to the best start, but now with the passing of time after Edith's death there has been a change. I am mindful of Sue's advice that I owe it to the people I have found not to turn my back on them. I am also mindful that forgiveness is not necessarily about the person who you feel has wronged you, but about you, the person wronged, being able to move forward without resentment and bitterness. I've given a lot more thought as to how my sudden appearance out of nowhere may have affected Sandra, and why she acted as she did. This is a woman who was to all intents and purposes abandoned by her mother. She was only 20 years old when Edith remarried and left the country, and her, behind. Granted, Sandra was a married woman and people did marry at a much younger age back then. She had a loving husband, but she also had a young daughter. You got on and you coped, that was the ethic of the day, but what young mother doesn't need family to be there for her, especially Mum? Edith upped sticks and left without a backward glance, and Sandra got on with her life because she had to. There is a core of inner strength there, a resilience, like her mother. For years after Edith left there was precious little of a meaningful relationship between the two women. Living overseas then seemed a whole lot further away than it is now, with Skype and Facebook and email and mobile phones. Back then, if you wanted to stay in touch, you wrote letters which you sent by Air Mail and if you were lucky you might be able to phone once in a while, if you had a phone because not everyone did. Often it was a terrible connection and maybe even a party line, with half of the neighbourhood listening in. And Edith didn't seem to want any kind of a connection with Sandra. Was it because of me? Was it because Sandra had a little girl that reminded her of me? Perhaps it wasn't about me at all because from what I have gleaned it seems what little connection the two of them had was always tenuous. According to Sandra, Edith would cut her off without a second thought if she had a mind to.

She and George both told me how Edith would play the two of them against each other, even as adults, one in favour, the other cut off, and then she would switch. George would retreat and have no contact with Edith and suddenly Sandra would be back in favour. It had only been in very recent years that there was some quality to the relationship that Sandra had with her mother. As Edith had grown older and more reliant on others, Sandra had felt that she finally had a useful place in her mother's life and was wanted (or at least needed), even if only at a distance on the other side of the world. I think Sandra had waited for years to have her mother respond to her in a positive way. And then, along came Perry. I think Sandra was afraid that if I were "in", she would again be "out". What a terrible thing for a daughter to fear. If I were to meet Edith and find favour, she could almost guarantee - as she herself put it - that she would be "out of the door". I had no idea of what was at stake when I was busy resenting her for not telling me where Edith was. Sandra told me that she felt she took a big risk when she asked Edith about me that day in the care home. The risk of having her mother tell her to leave, the risk of being cut off again and perhaps never being able to re-establish the relationship she had only recently managed to cultivate. If all this is true about the person Edith became, that was a big risk for her to take and I didn't fully appreciate it all at the time. There is nothing I can do now to change the past, and resentment doesn't help anyone. I do sincerely hope that Sandra and I can enrich each other's lives in the future.

My half-brother George passed away not too long ago. His alcoholism took a toll on his health and he died before I got to meet him in person. I have not yet met his daughter Emma, who is now married and has two young children, but it's on my list to get to Nebraska and meet them. I haven't met my other half-sister in America, Jean's younger sister

Carrie. The relationship between those two is not always good and there have been lengthy periods of time when they haven't spoken. Carrie isn't interested in meeting me or having any contact. She says she thinks I am an imposter but that makes little sense to me as I have nothing to gain by pretending to be a Gallagher. However, that is how it is, and I can't change it, but people and circumstances do change so I always have hope.

I would like one day to meet my other surviving aunts, and I've discovered a lot of cousins, too. Eugene was one of eight children and I believe they all had children of their own so that is a lot of cousins. I hope that the mystery of the photographs in Mama's Family Album will one day be solved, and I'm working on that. I understand from Jolene that many of the photographs have now been distributed to family members, so I hope they haven't been lost.

Has it all been worthwhile? Yes, it has. A resounding yes. I entitled the book The (Almost) Christmas Baby because the fact that Reggie and Eva Thurston took me in just before Christmas 1958, kept me and loved me, that I believe profoundly shaped my life more than anything else. I have always felt I was loved from the very beginning, despite being given up for adoption. I have never felt abandoned and I firmly believe that is down to them.

Appendix

Letter to Edith

3rd November 2009

Dear [Edith],

I hesitate to call you Mum, because that's not really who you are, although you are my mother we never knew each other. You died last week, and I never got the chance to meet you or speak with you; although I knew you were alive and in a Nursing Home in Las Vegas I was never sure exactly where but I had been planning to come and see you next May or June with your daughter [Sandra].

It's hard to know where to begin, really. I have always wondered about you. My mum and dad never hid from me that I was adopted, and they always told me I was loved more than any other child because they had REALLY wanted me, not being able to have children of their own. They didn't know very much about my history though, because Barnardo's kept everything secret in those days. They told me what they knew, which I suppose is what they had been told; that you had been a secretary on an air base and that my father was in the American Air Force and he had gone back to America before I was born.

When I was about 18 I went to Barnardo's and asked them questions. I went to Somerset House and got a copy of my original Birth Certificate. It had your full name on it, of course. My father's name wasn't on it, and Barnardo's wouldn't tell me who he was, just his first name, even though they admitted they had his full name in their file. They said they couldn't tell me unless you gave them your permission. They would have to contact you and ask. I wasn't ready for that, and I had it in my mind that you might have married someone else and not told your husband about me. I didn't want to ruin a new life, if you had one, and I didn't know if the news would be welcome so I decided to leave it alone for a while.

Barnardo's did tell me that I had a half-sister [Sandra] who was 18 years older who had married, and a half-brother [George] who was 8 years older. They gave me a typed A4 sheet with what struck me as a bit of a fairytale on it about how I had come to be given up for adoption. I lost the original they gave me years ago, but the main gist of it stuck in my mind.

I went to live in Canada in 1986, and while I was there I put myself on the Adoption Contact Register in the UK, in case someone out there was looking for me. I tried to find [George] several times, of course I didn't know he was in America. I thought he would probably still be [George Keyes] so he would be the easiest person to track down. I knew [Sandra] was married but I didn't know her married name. Although I had you in my mind, I thought that if I could find [George], there would be a safe buffer between us, and then if you didn't want contact I wouldn't pursue it. I wrote to all the [George Keyes] I could find in England, I don't think there were many, maybe 5. One very kind lady wrote back and said that her husband, [George Keyes] had recently passed away but that he wasn't who I was looking for. She wished me luck and success with my search. It was such a kind letter, I still have it.

I looked for you as well. Not necessarily to meet you, but to know who you were, what kind of life you had. I knew you were [Whittaker] before you were [Keyes] from my Birth Certificate, and I found an [Edith Whittaker] in Great Yarmouth. There was a [Sandra Keyes] living nearby. Great Yarmouth is where I was born of course, and on a trip back to England in 1988 I went to that street where [Edith Whittaker] lived and looked at the house. I wasn't brave enough to get out of the car and knock on the door. I know now that it wouldn't have been you, but at that time I couldn't have known, and I imagined it might have been you. I kicked myself for not knocking on that door every time I thought of it afterwards. I looked for the Log Cabin at Haddiscoe where you had stayed when you went to Norfolk to have me but it wasn't there. At least, I couldn't find it.

While I was in Canada I met and married my husband. We have two daughters who were both born out there, the oldest is now 14, and youngest is 13. They are both beautiful girls, but then I may be biased. They're your granddaughters. I wish you could have seen them. After I had my girls, I couldn't imagine being in the position you had been in, having to give a child up. There's such a natural bond between mother and child, I never understood it fully until I had my own. It broke my heart to think you had had to make that choice. I wondered then, on my birthday every year, whether you still thought of me and how on earth you had managed to pick up your life and go on. I never ever blamed you for the choice you made.

I always wondered, too, about my father. I knew his first name was [Eugene], and it was weird that honestly, somehow, when I first read the Barnardo's typed-out story with just his first name on it, I already knew it anyway. I knew he was an American, and from North Carolina. I thought it was Charlotte NC for some reason, I don't know why. I didn't really know where to start with looking for him. I remember years ago whilst in Canada writing to the American Embassy and asking them for information, and getting nowhere. I knew that the military records would be hard to access if not impossible, and really had nowhere to go unless I could find out his last name. Of course, Barnardo's had that in their records.

We came back to England in 2002. I knew that you were older than [Eugene], that you had been 38 when you had me so you would be in your 80's. Time was moving on so if I were going to try to find you I needed to get on with it before it was too late.

There had been a change in the law in England which meant that the information that Barnardo's held had to be given to me if I requested it. So I wrote to them and asked for it. I got put on a waiting list, but in February 2009 I went to their offices in Barkingside and was given my adoption file. It was fascinating to see your handwriting. You had signed all of those little slips when you sent money for my keep to

Barnardo's. You even wrote and asked them for a collection box to put in your office.

How times have changed. You had no support, financial or otherwise, it looks like you were just advised by the "Moral Welfare Worker" to have the baby and get back to your job as soon as possible. Which is exactly what you did. I can't say it didn't hurt when I read in the records how you left me with the Thurstons and went off back to Newbury with [George] almost straight away after leaving the hospital. I suppose that's the only way you could have done it though. No looking back. I thank God for the Thurstons, who cared for me and looked after me for six weeks before Mrs. Thurston took me on the train from Beccles to Paddington where Barnardo's travelling matron took me down to St. Christopher's in Tunbridge Wells where I stayed until I was adopted.

My name. Perry Christina. I came with the name, where did it come from? It was only you that could have answered that question. My mum and dad liked it, so they kept it. People ask me all the time, "What's it short for? That's an unusual name for a girl." I don't know the answer, and now I will never know. Who was this Perry, presumably I was named after someone or something that meant something to you? You must have cared to have given me such a special name.

Thank God for the Internet. When I went looking, I still couldn't find [George] anywhere, or you, and I couldn't understand it. Of course, now I know you married [Roy] and went off to America in 1961. I did find [Sandra], and I also found [Jean] her daughter. I wrote to both of them. I wasn't 100% sure I was right, but they were both in the Newbury area which is where you had lived. [Jean] phoned me and told me I had the right person. She also told me that you were alive and living in America, and that [Sandra] needed some time to adjust before she spoke to me. [Sandra] rang me the same night, though. I was elated to think you were still alive. I hadn't expected it. She wouldn't tell me where you were. She said something like, "You don't know what she's like. She's a nasty and cruel person, really." I didn't know what to say. I can't say that's what I expected to hear, anyway. She also said she couldn't or wouldn't tell me where you were. She said she wanted to protect you. None of it made sense to me then, and it still doesn't if I'm honest. When I pressed her about where you were, she said, "Well, it's a big place. She's in a Nursing Home in Las Vegas." She told me that [George] was in rehab in Nebraska.

I phoned [George] and spoke to him. He remembered going to Norfolk with you before I was born. He remembered staying in a caravan and that there were railway carriages there. He hadn't known about me. Neither had [Sandra], although she had had some suspicion from something that [George] had said to an Aunty, years ago, about ladies getting fat when they have babies. I suppose I have been a bit of a shock to both of them.

When I met [Sandra] last March she showed me a photo of you, and your husband [Roy], and [George]. It was a black and white framed print, probably taken in the early 1960's just before you went to America to start your new life. You were on the far right, next to [Roy], and [George] on the left. [Roy] was wearing his uniform, it struck me what a kind looking man he was. I looked at your face, and I thought, "I know this person. She looks like someone I know, so familiar." I remember staring at you for what seemed like several minutes, just racking my brains from where I had seen you before. And then it struck me, how stupid of me. Of course I knew your face. You are my mother. I've seen you before. That was a weird feeling, I don't think I will ever forget it.

I feel I have had the right to meet you denied me. I also feel you have had the right to meet me, and your grandchildren, denied you. I am struggling with this. I am trying hard not to blame [Sandra] but she has steadfastly stood in the way, saying she wanted to protect you. I suspect she even told the nursing home not to allow me to have contact with you. She told me she asked you whether the name Perry meant anything to you, when she went out to see you in May this year. She said you didn't remember me. She said you had said, "Me? Have a baby out of wedlock? Who would say such a thing." She said she thought you were telling the truth because you didn't remember about [Arthur], either. He was your baby boy who died, before you had [George].

I blame myself, too. I should have pushed [Sandra] harder, made her understand how important this was to me. I wanted to give her time to adjust. That's what she said she wanted. She said she may not always feel that way, and so I waited. When you said you didn't remember, I asked [Sandra] again where you were. I said I wanted to see you. How could it do any harm if you didn't remember? She said she thought it was best that your secret died with you. You had kept the secret all those years, who were we to dredge it up? She even swore [Emma], [George's] daughter, to secrecy.

[Sandra] came here with [Henry] in September for a weekend. I wrongly thought she had changed her mind and was going to tell me about you, because she had rung and said she had done some thinking, and that none of this was her fault, or mine. It was yours. But that wasn't it at all; I misunderstood. She wanted to tell me that she didn't feel guilty any more about not telling me. I wanted to scream at her, you don't understand! I've come all this way and now there's no ending. When I tried to tell her I needed some closure, she said perhaps I could meet her and [Henry] in Las Vegas next year and she'd take me to see you. That was the only way she could see it happening. I had already saved up enough for the flight. And now you've gone. I don't even have anywhere to send this letter, but I have to write it down, and get it all out. I don't want to be bitter towards [Sandra], I am praying that God gives me grace to understand, but it's hard. There's a part of me that resents her for keeping me away from you.

I want you to know that I did try to find you. I found out your last name. I spent hours on the computer looking for you. One night I phoned every single Nursing Home that I could find in Las Vegas, but I couldn't find you. I found the condo you and [Roy] used to live in, near to the Walmart on Tropicana. There was a care home across the road called Montara Meadows, and I thought that's where you must have been. I contacted them and first they said, no, then when I tried again they said you had been there but didn't live there any more. I didn't believe them. I think [Sandra] told them not to give me any information. Is that where you died?

I so wanted to see you. I didn't care if you couldn't remember me, I just wanted to see you for myself, to say hello and hold your hand. If I could have told you that I never blamed you, you did the right thing, I had a great life, then that would have been a bonus. I would have had a memory of my own, rather than only knowing you through the eyes of other people. Do you know, I told my mum all about my search for you. She said she would like to have thanked you for giving me up, that you gave her and my dad the chance of a life they would never have had without me. That without people like you, people like them would never have the chance for a family of their own, children and grandchildren.

[Eugene's] family knew there was a daughter in England. They told me that he came back to see you some time after he had got out of the Air Force. There's a picture in their Family Album of him with you. I think it must be you. Also a picture of a little girl aged 2 or 3. I haven't seen those pictures yet, but I can't quite understand how he got a picture of me because I had been adopted by then. His sister [Roseanne] told me that you were at his house in Red Springs in 1963, and that he picked you up from Raleigh-Durham Airport in 1974. Was that really you? Did you still see him? I have so many questions that may never be answered now. Did you know he died in 1978?

Well, I think I am done. I don't know how to grieve for you because I never knew you. How can you lose someone you never had? I am so sorry I never had the chance to thank you for what you gave me. You had a very difficult life from what I know. I think your mother died when you were young. You lost a baby, you had a very difficult marriage, fled with your children and little else, and tried to start a new life. You got pregnant and gave up a baby for adoption. Those are all such life changing events, you must have been a very strong person to have dealt with all those things on your own. [Sandra] said you didn't believe in God, but I have wondered whether in those difficult times you ever cried out to Him.

Maybe you just cursed Him, or found it easier not to believe in Him. I don't think I could have gotten through all this without Him, I believe He has guided me in my search and that He has a purpose in all of this. I am sorry that His plan did not include us meeting, for whatever reason best known to Him.

I find it so sad that there was no funeral, no flowers, no goodbyes; just a cremation which [Sandra] said is what you wanted. Nothing to mark your passing. I can't believe a person can live for 89 years and not have touched the lives of others. There must be people out there who knew you and cared for you. You never knew me, but you have always been there in my heart and on some level I have loved you all my life. I wanted you to know that. It doesn't have to be reciprocated, it's enough that it is there.

Many of these are thoughts that even if I had met you would probably have remained unspoken, but it has helped me to write them down and given me some peace. Thank you for giving me life.

Your daughter,

Perry